"Now it's here—a book that c
thoroughly explains the forces of
and stringent logic in her appro
writing, the author leads us right to u..
You will be fascinated and stimulated to create, nu.
individual personal brand."
Edgar C. Britschgi, MA/MBA, President of the British Swiss Chamber of Commerce, Zurich/London; Managing Partner, Combo Management AG, Zug, New York, Shanghai, Taipei, Tel Aviv

"This book is an excellent read for corporate leaders who want to message their connection to the corporate brand and its stakeholders. Stories make the bonds which are critical in today's business world. Use Martin's "D" method: DISCOVER, DEVELOP, DISTILL, DIGITIZE, DISSEMINATE, DISCLOSE, DOCUMENT, and DESIGN, to create the stories that message your unique skills and personal qualities most effectively."
Amy Chen, General Manager, L'Oréal, Taiwan

"Posting your "story" to use Bernadette's term, is key, not only for closed communities such as associations and company intranets like EPWN and The Greater IBM Connection, but for publicly viewed sites like Viadeo and LinkedIn. Her book provides the direction, guidance, tips, and tools to get you started."
Christine Cluzel - Manager of Marketing and Strategy - IBM Global Financing France
European Professional Women's Network (EPWN) - Member

"For chefs, aspiring chefs and all who are ensconced in the culinary world and passionate about what they do...sometimes the hardest thing is to market, promote, and brand yourself...yet we all have an interesting and different story. In her book, Bernadette Martin explains the importance of storytelling and crafting the Branded BIO tool...a good start for chefs launching their career."

Chef Kyle Shadix, Certified Chef de Cuisine, Registered Dietitian/Nutritionist, Author, Speaker, Spokesperson

"They say a picture is worth a thousand words—well, this book is a fantastic resource to help you paint your own personal picture."

Kip Harrell, President, MBA Career Services Council; Associate Vice President Career and Professional Development, Thunderbird School of Global Management

"Years of hard work leave us with stories to tell. Whether you're a 'digital native' or a 'digital virgin,' Bernadette Martin helps you make a brand out of these stories...your brand. I had the pleasure and luck of working with the author parallel to her writing this book. Applying her insights as I tested my story, she guided my own 'brand in the making.'"

Mathias Herrmann, Managing Director (DG), Mercedes Benz Financial Services, France

"I often use storytelling as an entry point into new cultures I need to explore. It creates a powerful bridge between who I am and the audience. I now have a brand new tool to help me in this exercise. I am delighted to have discovered Bernadette Martin's book."

Silvia Cambié, Member of the Executive Board, IABC (International Association of Business Communicators); Director, Chanda Communications; author, 'International Communications Strategy,' nominated for the FT Goldman Sachs Awards

More Praise on Page 147

Storytelling about Your Brand Online & Offline

A Compelling Guide to Discovering Your Story

By Bernadette Martin
Foreword by William Arruda
Afterword by Jason Alba

20660 Stevens Creek Blvd., Suite 210
Cupertino, CA 95014

First Printing: July 2010
Paperback ISBN: 978-1-60005-144-9 (1-60005-144-8)
eBook ISBN: 978-1-60005-145-6 (1-60005-145-6)
Place of Publication: Silicon Valley, California, USA
Paperback Library of Congress Number: 2010927970

Trademarks

Warning and Disclaimer

Dedication

To my brand extension, Natalie Anela.
Je t'aime.

Acknowledgments

I would like to acknowledge all of the contributors, whose perspectives and insights are greatly appreciated. In particular, Sue Brettell who penned the visual guidelines section, including an amazing BIO makeover. She also created the cover design and gave me her valuable support and advice on design in general. Megan Fitzgerald, who contributed to the section on Internationalizing your BIO, with three of her clients featured. Lynda Sydney, who contributed to the writing guidelines section, offering a host of tips and tools. As well I would like to thank my editor, Cathy Altman Nocquet, whose direction gave clarity and structure to my book when it was starting to take on multiple lives. *Merci mille fois* for reining it in!

The BIOs of all contributors, including the more than 20 stellar experts and recruiters I interviewed can be found at **http://www.visibilitybranding.com**.

Note to the Reader

I want to thank all the people who are not messaging their brand or telling their story effectively. It gave me a reason to write this book. To use Paul Harvey's quote, I help clients to tell the "rest of the story" meaning what they don't realize is impressive, unique and amazing about themselves. Call it viral marketing or word of mouth (WOM), if you tell a good story it will grow exponentially as more and more people are impressed and want to pass it on. This book will give you a fresh perspective on how to trigger the stories and create GEMS that will delight your target, make you "talkable," and create long lasting ambassadors for the "Brand Called You." Never underestimate the power of a good story and the big question (you can wait to answer once you read this book):
What's Your Story???

Tribute to Paul Harvey (1918–2009), a Legendary Storyteller

Paul Harvey was an American radio broadcaster famous for his "The Rest of the Story" segments that had an audience of 24 million people a week. The most noticeable features of Harvey's idiosyncratic delivery were his dramatic pauses, quirky intonation, and his famous tag line...the rest of the story.

And his story...son of a policeman who was murdered when Harvey was three; Paul Harvey made radio receivers as a young boy. Impressed by his voice, a high school teacher encouraged him to apply at the local radio station. His first job was sweeping the floors, but soon he was filling in on the air, reading commercials and the news. Eventually, this led to a stellar career as a radio station director, roving reporter for leading news stations, broadcaster, and commentator. His own talk show *Harvey's News and Comment* was streamed on the Web twice a day and featured on 1,200 radio stations and in 300 newspapers.

For Gen Y'ers, X'ers and Baby Boomers...listen to his legendary voice that captivated many...weaving stories that drew you in, kept you hanging and wrapped up with momentous splendor. http://www.youtube.com/watch?v=jivF03JahHU

My Dad introduced me to Paul Harvey when I was a little girl and we shared a love of his storytelling. Our conversations later in life, no matter where I lived, often included "Did you hear Paul Harvey's story today?" Thanks, Dad.

A Message from Happy About®

Thank you for your purchase of this Happy About book. It is available online at **http://happyabout.com/storytelling.php** or at other online and physical bookstores.

- Please contact us for quantity discounts at **sales@happyabout.info**
- If you want to be informed by email of upcoming Happy About® books, please email **bookupdate@happyabout.info**

Happy About is interested in you if you are an author who would like to submit a non-fiction book proposal or a corporation that would like to have a book written for you. Please contact us by email **editorial@happyabout.info** or phone (1-408-257-3000).

Other Happy About books available include:

- Red Fire Branding:
  http://www.happyabout.com/redfirebranding.php
- The Successful Introvert:
  http://happyabout.info/thesuccessfulintrovert.php
- I'm in a Job Search—Now What???:
  http://www.happyabout.com/jobsearchnowwhat.php
- I'm at a Networking Event—Now What???:
  http://www.happyabout.com/networking-event.php
- I'm on Facebook—Now What???:
  http://www.happyabout.com/facebook.php
- I'm on LinkedIn—Now What???:
  http://www.happyabout.com/linkedinhelp.php
- 42 Rules to Jumpstart Your Professional Success:
  http://www.42rules.com/jump_start_professional_success/
- 42 Rules for Effective Connections:
  http://www.happyabout.com/42rules/effectiveconnections.php
- 42 Rules for 24-Hour Success on LinkedIn:
  http://www.happyabout.com/42rules/24hr-success-linkedin.php
- Rule #1: Stop Talking!:
  http://www.happyabout.com/listenerspress/stoptalking.php
- Twitter Means Business:
  http://www.happyabout.com/twitter/tweet2success.php
- Communicating the American Way:
  http://www.happyabout.com/communicating-american-way.php

Contents

Foreword by William Arruda

It took technology—Web 2.0—to make executives and employees at all levels of the organization acknowledge that business truly is a human endeavor. It's clear that, to succeed today, we need to build relationships inside and outside the company, regardless of our role or level in the organization. We must create emotional connections with all members of our brand community—in person and through social media. Communication is the currency of these connections.

Neurological research along with our own experience tells us that storytelling is an extremely powerful form of communication. Because stories combine facts, figures and details with emotions, colors and imagery, they create synapses between the left and right halves of your brain. This makes stories memorable. Being memorable is critical in a world where we are bombarded with millions of stimuli every day.

Telling your story is essential to your success and professional fulfillment and an important element of the Reach personal branding process; it makes your personal brand come alive by allowing you to express your key attributes, values, passions, and accomplishments in a relevant and compelling way. Yet you may be like many of the executives and corporate clients I work with who find telling their story a challenge. Knowing where to start, what to include and how to convey their brand is not obvious. That's where this book comes in.

Storytelling about Your Brand Online & Offline is replete with tips, tools, resources, and examples that will help you gain clarity on what you want to say and how you can deliver it through the power of storytelling. In this book, Bernadette Martin practices what she preaches, using fun and engaging stories to guide you through the process so you can captivate your target audience with stories that highlight what makes you interesting, attractive and exceptional.

Bernadette is the right person to tell this story. I have known her for years. She was among the first to complete my Personal Branding Certification Program in France and quickly developed this very important niche that sits at the intersection of personal branding and storytelling. Her steadfast focus on brand-building through storytelling has made her a sought-after consultant for individuals, organizations, and universities connected to some of the world's most important brands: Cisco, Mercedes, Chanel, Orange, Publicis Groupe, DBM, Cordon Bleu, INSEAD, Thunderbird, IMD, American University of Paris and HEC.

As the public demands greater transparency from corporate executives, and leaders recognize that they must be more visible and available to their stakeholders, storytelling will become a core leadership development skill. Executives and professionals throughout the organization will need to become adroit storytellers and expert at using the right tools for getting those stories to their target audience. Video is one of those tools.

In my top personal branding trends for 2010, I predicted that video will have the greatest impact on the personal branding landscape this year and for years to come. Video is the future of personal branding and it also happens to be the perfect vehicle for telling your story. Recognizing this, Bernadette includes everything you need to know about using this medium effectively. The advice she provides will enable you to gain a competitive edge by incorporating video into your storytelling strategy.

Throughout this book, Bernadette expertly fuses theory with practical advice to help people and corporations access and express their most compelling stories to strengthen their brands. Your story is only 150 pages away. *What are you waiting for?*

William Arruda
Founder, Reach Communications

Part I: The Power of Storytelling

Across cultures and languages, storytelling is a powerful communication tool, in both personal and business contexts. Psychologist Susan Weinschenk confirms the effectiveness of storytelling as supported by neurological research. A Mind Map, which engages both the rational and intuitive sides of your brain, illustrates how the sections of this book inter-relate, but feel free to reap the benefits in any order. The world will be listening to the stories that arise! Stakeholders are more eager than ever to discover the personal brands behind corporate leadership. Techniques of personal branding follow, using the Reach personal branding process and the Visibility Branding "D-words." You will DISCOVER and DEVELOP your stories, DISTILL the ones that resonate with your target, DIGITIZE and then DISCLOSE and DISSEMINATE online and offline. Finally, you will DOCUMENT and DESIGN with your unique visual branding. An example of a personal revelation about the power of storytelling ends Part I.

- Introduction
- Mind Map

- Neuro Research and Storytelling
- Storytelling about the "Brand Called You"
- Product Brand Storytelling
- Corporate, NGO, and Non-Profit Storytelling
- Corporate Leadership Storytelling
- Personal Brand Storytelling
- The Reach Personal Brand Process
- A Personal Story

Introduction

nce upon a time...these words were probably your favorite as a child...was it when you were in your flannel pajamas, all ready for bed, with mom or dad waiting to tuck you in? You had a book picked out, or better yet, they had a story from their childhood. But wait a minute. You picked up this book thinking you were going to get great tips, tools, and advice on how to craft your professional story as you may be in career transition mode, or a recent graduate...or maybe you want to attract clients, partners and investors. So what's the segue from flannel pajamas to your career needs and challenges? Hang on...it's coming...but first in PART I, let's set the stage, and establish the power of storytelling. In PART II, you will learn how to extract your stories; in PART III and PART IV, you will learn where to tell your stories online and offline and finally, in Part V, in a more practical and tactile sense, you will learn how to write your professional story and incorporate your unique visual branding with lots of tips, tools, resources and guidelines to make it compelling to your target. Fully aware of the power of storytelling and to keep you engaged, many stories have been woven into the various chapters to give you examples and ideas. You will see...going from flannel pajamas to career storytelling is not such a stretch.

Mind Map

For those of you who are more visual in nature, here is a Mind Map of the book which engages and stimulates both your right and left brain. The logical connections, lines and words will attract your left 'logical' brain whereas the colors, pictures, and smooth flowing curves will engage your right 'pictorial/visual' brain. This Mind Map gives you an overview of the information content and the inter-relationships of the various chapters, so you get a sense of how it all works together. However, you do not need to read this book sequentially. You can make your way through the theoretical and practical information which follows, as fits your needs.

For better viewing of Mind Map go to http://visibilitybranding.fr/blog/.

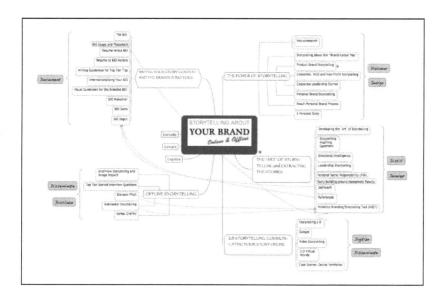

Neuro Research and Storytelling

Storytelling has been around since the beginning of time. It was the primary medium for passing along culture, history, lore and lessons learned. Even today, anthropologists claim that 70% of everything we learn is through stories. So what is the definition of "story?"

Its basic framework is a beginning, middle and end. Ideally, a story would have a stimulating beginning, an engaging middle, and a decisive yet compelling ending that leaves the listener wanting to hear more. And, going beyond that, a POWERFUL and MEMORABLE story would trigger the senses and evoke emotion, creating a connection between the narrator and the listener. Stories can indicate a conflict, character development, resolution, or transformation. There may be a protagonist, an earth shattering journey, or a surprising conclusion. These are all ways of strengthening the message. But for our purposes, we'll keep the definition simple: A story is an expression of real and imagined experiences, *i.e.*, fictional and non-fictional, shaped, crafted and woven by the storyteller in a sensory fashion. It could play out in an oral, written, visual or tactical context, in a book, movie, poem, theater, comic book, song, dance, cartoon, epic, prose, ballad...resume, elevator pitch, biography, video, LinkedIn profile, blog, website, Facebook, Twitter, YouTube, newsletter...now, the segue is becoming clear.

A story is an expression of real and imagined experiences *i.e.*, **fictional and non-fictional, that are shaped, crafted and woven by the storyteller in a sensory fashion.**

Research indicates that across cultures and languages the first most commonly uttered words by children include the word "story." Hence the meaning behind the cover of this book. Neurological research validates the amazing power of storytelling. In fact, scientific evidence establishes that story learning may enhance memory retention up to seven-fold. Remembering with stories is easier than remembering sentences, word lists and bullet points followed by a host of action verbs. Psychologist Susan Weinschenk, confirms the effectiveness of storytelling as supported by neurological research, noting that our brains are *WIRED* to process information as stories. This allows us to process large amounts in small chunks, what she calls "event structure perception," and store it effectively in memory. More importantly, it helps us to connect *EMOTIONALLY* with another person. This is developed further by Susan's contribution on this subject, which follows and sets the stage for the rest of this book.

Storytelling about the "Brand Called You"

As this ever happened to you? You are listening to a speaker give a presentation. The topic is kind of interesting to you, but you find your attention starting to wander, and then the speaker says, "Let me tell you a story about the time...." Suddenly you perk up, ready to hear the story.

Since humans have used words to communicate, they've been telling stories that capture and hold our attention. They convey facts, but they also convey emotions and feelings and allow us to better process information.

A story is a written, spoken, poetic, prose, graphic, sung, acted, or danced construction that describes a sequence of fictional or non-fictional events. It can describe a character over time, and that character, of course, can be you.

When we hear the word *story*, we may think of an adult reading a book to a group of little children sitting in a circle, or a professional "storyteller" relating a story using dramatic voices and gestures. But we are all storytellers. Re-create in your mind a typical day, and think about your interactions with your friends, family, and colleagues throughout the day. At breakfast you tell your wife or husband about a dream you had (story). When you get to work you tell a colleague about the traffic accident you saw on the highway (story). You meet a friend for lunch and tell them about the frustrating meeting you had that morning at work (story) and about the holiday you are planning on taking in a few weeks (story). If you think about it, you will realize that most of your communications, whether "professional or personal," are stories.

Stories allow us to process large amounts of information in small, understandable chunks. Recent research by Nicole Speer (2007) shows that the brain uses stories to process and store information in small chunks. Psychologists call this chunking of parts of a story *event structure perception*.

In Speer's research, participants read narratives about everyday activities and, while they were reading, had their brain activity monitored using functional Magnetic Resonance Imaging (fMRI). The pattern of activity in the fMRI scan mimicked the pattern of the story. There would be a burst of activity, then a pause, then another burst, then another pause, and so on.

A few days later the participants came back and read the same narratives, but this time they did not get the fMRI scan. Instead they marked the story—they were asked to mark the different "chunks" of the story. In research terminology the participants were marking *event boundaries*—the beginning and end points of points in the narrative.

When Speer compared the fMRI brain pictures to the chunking the participants had marked, they matched. The event boundaries occurred when there was a transition in the story, such as a change in location or a different character. The brain was processing the story in chunks.

When we read a story or listen to someone tell a story, we are processing the story in many parts of our brains. If the story is being told then the auditory parts of our brain, that process sound, are active. If we are reading the story, then the part of our brain that processes text is active. Research also shows us that when we listen or read a story we are imagining the visual scenes, so the visual processing of our brain is active.

The latest research (Singer 2004) reveals that the emotional parts of our brains are also active. Singer first took pictures of participants' brains while they were experiencing pain. She discovered that there are some parts of the brain that process where in the body the pain is located, and make a determination of how intense the pain is. I have dubbed this the "objective pain center." Other parts of the brain separately process how unpleasant the pain feels, and how bothersome it is at the moment. We'll call this the "subjective pain center."

Singer next asked the participants to read stories about people experiencing pain. When participants read stories about someone in pain, the objective pain centers were quiet, but the subjective pain centers were active. Stories about others invoke empathy, as we imagine what it is like to be them.

So stories not only allow us to process information and store it effectively in memory, but also, perhaps most importantly, they let us connect emotionally with another person.

Singer, T., B. Seymour, J. O'Doherty, H. Kaube, J.D. Dolan, and C. Frith. 2004. Empathy for pain involves the affective but not sensory component of pain. Science 303: 1157–1162.

Speer, Nicole K., Jeffrey M. Zacks, and Jeremy R. Reynolds. 2007. Human brain activity time-locked to narrative event boundaries. Psychological Science, Vol. 18(5), 449–455.

Read Susan's BIO at http://www.visibilitybranding.com or on her blog http://www.whatmakesthemclick.net.

Product Brand Storytelling

efore delving into storytelling about personal brands, let's clearly draw the link to storytelling about corporate, product and service brands. The whole phenomenon, which some even call a "movement," around Personal Branding started with an article written in 1997 by Tom Peters. Entitled the "Brand Called You," it appeared in Fast Company Magazine and still resonates today. After my career of 15 years working with corporate and product brands such as Proctor & Gamble, DHL, Ford, Nestlé, American Express, KLM and others, Peters' idea of applying the same tools and methodologies to "people" brands made perfect sense. The transition to personal branding that came a few years later was a natural.

> **The American Marketing Association defines a brand as the image, perception, or story created from the accumulation of sensory, emotional and rational touch points one has with the product (this could be a person, place or thing).**

The strength of a brand is based on the stories people relate about their experiences, assumptions, and judgments. Brand stories are designed to create emotions like desire, craving, and trust to win the hearts and minds of customers. Taking this a step further, when we talk about our experiences, the touch points (the good, the bad, and the ugly) of this "word of mouth" communication is storytelling. We talk about and "spread the word" about experiences that move us...which could be in an upsetting, unexpected, or delightful way.

When was the last time you went on and on about a product that you found "okay" or "fine" or "adequate" or "fit the bill?" Instead we tend to talk about the brands that exceed our expectations or disappoint. The most innovative, remarkable and memorable brands are rooted in sensory, emotional and rational stimulation. Louis Vuitton, Apple, MAC, Hello Kitty, Subway, Ben & Jerry's, Duracell—there are strong, compelling, and unique stories behind these brands that resonate with the respective target. Assets, inventory, physical goods, balance sheet results...these are all the tangibles, but they only represent 40% of a company's value. Research from the top consulting companies indicate that the remaining 60% is based on "intangibles" i.e., the brand image or perception that creates competitive advantage. Stories have equity.

Corporate, NGO, and Non-Profit Storytelling

orporate, NGO, and Non-Profit storytelling plays a key role in messaging an organization's values and purpose. Companies put out an official statement of their mission, but it is really the stories that people tell, the stakeholders' stories, that have the most impact. Most organizations have a written set of values such as integrity, professionalism, innovation, exceptional customer service, achieving the impossible, encouraging individualism, and creativity. It is key that stakeholders understand these values, and stories make them come to life.

Here is how values translate into stories, using Walt Disney as an example.

The Walt Disney Company Values:

- Nurturing and promulgation of "wholesome American values"
- Creativity, dreams and imagination
- Fanatical attention to consistency and detail
- Preservation and control of the Disney magic

The employees at Disney are called "cast members" and are trained to address children at their level. This means the "cast member" who is sweeping the streets of the Magic Kingdom to keep them impeccable, will bend down to answer a question from a five-year-old. This little story, seemingly inconsequential, captures the enactment of a Disney value. Strong brands have enduring values with a clear purpose and are lived by their employees.

"Corporate Storytelling" as a term is making its way into the vernacular, and is no longer a "buzz" word. Corporations want to learn which stories resonate, and which ones need to be told. To this end, companies conduct highly structured brand audits, working with an external agency or consultants. Holding focus groups with key audience stakeholders is one step, and permits the identification of perceptual gaps and lost opportunities related to the corporate story. Also referred to as the Brand

Blueprint, this 360 degree approach reveals findings that include strategic positioning, messaging, audience profiling and specific marketing tactics. The brand audit helps companies discover and tell their most strategic story, as well as engage employees and stakeholders (creditors, customers, directors, government, owners, shareholders, suppliers, unions, and the community) to make them "brand ambassadors."

Corporate Leadership Storytelling

"Mastering the art of storytelling for an executive is a good way to 'sell' his profile and career plans. I write mini-BIOs for candidates in order to introduce their CV to other HR professionals or top managers who pay attention to short and targeted information."
- Sandrine Joseph, Talent Management Director

With the surge of new social media opportunities and the need and desire from stakeholders for transparency, a new area is developing around personal branding for the leaders, also known as the Executive Team, Board of Directors or Founders, behind corporate brands. Coupled with a certain "right to know" and a touch of natural curiosity, stakeholders now expect corporations to offer a more transparent view of the people at their helms. This applies to enterprises that are consumer centric as well as B2B, NGOs, and non-profits.

Most corporate sites provide at least the names of the top managers. Some go further and post BIOS or photos. Now, with the explosive growth of 2.0 technology, and video in particular, forward thinking companies are paying more attention to the personal brands and images of their leaders. A vast array of creative and innovative media opportunities exist to message their stories. While adding value, this communication also lends an emotional, human element to the corporate brand. If well-messaged and clear, it will have a positive and brand building impact. Alignment of the Corporate Brand Story and the Personal Brand Story of the leaders is key. Not only do executives have their own blogs and Twitter accounts, video also plays a huge role. Working with a personal brand consultant and a professional video photographer is increasingly the norm.

Personal Brand Storytelling

ersonal Branding is passionate work. It's an intensive process that helps people recognize, leverage and communicate the real "GEMS" in their backgrounds. In this book you will learn how to build a body of stories that will reveal your values, emotional intelligence and leadership skills. Stories that message and transmit your qualities, attributes, talents and positive lessons learned. Storytelling is an excellent way to convey value. In working with individual clients, my process starts with an interview process called the "intake" session. Story time! Pointed questions are asked, copious notes are taken, and stories start to flow. It's important to pick up on nuggets that are often brushed over, to elaborate and develop. It may be surprising...most people are not aware of what makes them unique. What are your "intangibles?" What are the stories that will make you "talkable" and create brand ambassadors that will spread the word about the "Brand Called You?"

An effective coach can act as a conduit for interesting story angles, and help you elicit, craft and connect stories. Whether you work through some of the questions, tools, and exercises yourself or with a partner, stories that "delight" your target and make you "talkable" will start to take shape. Along the way, this can create "accidental" spokespeople. You will become more than just a commodity that you may appear as on your resume. Identities, beliefs and values live and breathe in a matrix of stories. What is important is to make it clear and show how everything is connected. It's all about the stories.

In communicating your professional experience you have to be an expert at marketing yourself. Unfortunately, even people who are marketers by profession struggle with this. They may be brilliant at marketing products or services, but when it comes to marketing themselves, they are lost. It's far more difficult than it sounds.

There are three common reasons why most people do not communicate their accomplishments effectively. First, they are not clear about what makes them unique. Second, even if they are lucid about this, they are not sure how to articulate it or choose the right media mix to reach their target. Third, they are unable to make themselves "talkable" and create brand ambassadors within their networks. The result is an enormous number of missed opportunities to communicate their capabilities. It comes down to this: they are not good storytellers. They may need outside feedback from a coach for their stories to surface and take an appropriate structure, as well as to develop an effective networking strategy and attitude.

The Reach Personal Brand Process

"What Makes You Unique, Makes You Successful."
- William Arruda, Reach Communications

Certification as a Reach Personal Brand Strategist is grounded in the 3-step process of EXTRACT, EXPRESS and EXUDE, as developed by William Arruda, Founder of Reach, and considered to be the "Personal Branding Guru." The Visibility Branding Storytelling process dovetails nicely with the Reach process and can be used as an overlay. The Visibility Branding "D-words," listed below, are positioned throughout the book to help you perfect the stories that will make the most of your brand.

- DISCOVER your stories with provocative and inspiring questions
- DEVELOP your stories using assessments and external feedback
- DISTILL your stories that will resonate with your target
- DIGITIZE your stories considering the latest 2.0 technology
- DISCLOSE your stories effectively
- DISSEMINATE your stories to your target online and offline
- DOCUMENT your stories by writing them down with clarity
- DESIGN your stories into a coherent structure and with visual branding

The Reach personal branding process is further explained in the book *Career Distinction* by William Arruda and Kirsten Dixson. As references are made to the Reach Personal Branding Process it is important to have a clear definition up front. Not wanting to re-create the wheel, here in William's words, the three phases are defined:

EXTRACT PHASE: In the first step in successful personal branding, you unearth your unique promise of value—your brand. This is the most important and reflective phase in the branding process because it reveals the core around which you will build your brand. You uncover your authentic brand by identifying your vision, purpose, values, passions and your unique strengths and differentiation. You discover what others think about you, and identify the competitive landscape and your target audience.

EXPRESS PHASE: In this phase you identify the ideal combination of online and offline communication tools to reach your audience effectively, while ensuring that you are standing out among the numerous others who are offering seemingly similar services.

EXUDE PHASE: In this phase you develop a strategy for making your brand visible to those who need to know about you so that you can achieve your goals. In other words, you design a way to compellingly communicate your personal brand. To communicate most effectively, you need to align your brand environment—that is, everything that surrounds you—with your personal brand.

A Personal Story

How I Discovered the Power of Storytelling

As a Tour Director (TD) with Tauck World Discovery, a leading high end international tour operator, my primary responsibility was to impart knowledge and give commentary about the flora, fauna and history of the areas we visited. My itineraries included the Canadian Rockies, Hawaii and the southwestern United States. I bought and enthusiastically perused numerous books about these areas and quickly attained a high level of attachment at many levels.

Part of my TD training entailed going on a tour twice as a "student" and learning from seasoned TDs, each having their respective styles and ways of imparting information. In traveling through these gorgeous areas TDs had a captive audience, sometimes as many as 45 in the coach. Some TDs, more left brain in nature, would expound factually on the elevation of the peaks, plate tectonics, precipitation and glacier recession statistics. Observing the captive audience, one would see mouths starting to gape, not in awe of the amazing facts and figures presented but rather because they were falling asleep catching ZZZs. The more courteous, feeling the onslaught of slumber, would put on their sunglasses and comfortably close their eyes behind dark shades! Not only were they taking expensive naps, but they were missing out on some amazing fabulous scenery. All Tauck TDs were not fact and figure oriented, as some of the best storytelling techniques came from colleagues. However, I made a personal commitment to perfect the art of storytelling and to continuously weave engaging and captivating stories that would make these places come alive. Eventually having my own groups and giving commentary, my clients still heard about seismic activity and glacier retreat but it was "cache" to use a French term, or cloaked in stories.

How did this play out on the various tours? In Hawaii the stories I wove were about Pele, the goddess of fire and lightning. Her home was believed to be the fire pit at the summit caldera of one of the Earth's most continually active volcanoes. The lava flows and volcanic activity were easily explained by her violent temper that revolved around stories of seduction and jealousy. Many of Pele's rivals and lovers were not lucky enough to escape with their lives and were the target of hurled molten lava. Guess what? The guests were riveted, awake *and* learning about diverging and converging plate tectonics.

On the tours in the Canadian Rockies, the wildlife, weather, flora, and fauna were a backdrop to the stories about Wild Bill Peyto. He came from England in 1886 at the age of 18 to work on building the Canadian Pacific Railroad and later became an outfitter, guide, trapper, prospector, and Park Warden as well as serving in WWI. Stories abound around this colorful character, his wild antics and wicked sense of humor.

On the Southwest tours, stories about the Hopi Indians, their dances, ceremonies, art, and cuisine illuminated the composition of the earth and indigenous vegetation. Looking back at this seven year stint, this was a career of a professional storyteller. Yes...lesson learned...stories are powerful.

Part II: The "Art" of Storytelling and Extracting the Stories

"Their story, yours and mine— it's what we all carry with us on this trip we take, and we owe it to each other to respect our stories and learn from them."
William Carlos Williams

DISCOVER * DEVELOP * DISTILL*
*DIGITIZE * DISSEMINATE * DISCLOSE **
*DOCUMENT * DESIGN*

Part II launches your storytelling adventure with provocative questions that help you develop solid and original content. Assessments, exercises and tools reveal your Emotional Intelligence (EQ), leadership skills, key attributes and strengths. Story "GEMS" surface to be woven into your written and verbal storytelling, using quotes, humor, childhood memories, and more. DEVELOP and DISTILL compelling stories that will resonate with your target, using the Visibility Branding Storytelling Tool (VBST). Prepare your stories to use during interviews and introductions. Build storied content from external sources: reference letters, evaluations, and the amazing 360°Reach assessment tool. Finally, acquire tips, etiquette, and strategy on requesting and giving recommendations for your Personal Brand Toolkit.

- The "Art" of Storytelling

- Storytelling Inspiring Questions

- Emotional Intelligence (EQ) Stories

- Leadership Storytelling

- Personal Social Responsibility (PSR) Stories

- Story Building around Assessment Results

- The 360°Reach Assessment

- References

- The Visibility Branding Storytelling Tool (VBST)

The "Art" of Storytelling

As you learn to EXTRACT the stories (structure comes later) those emotional and rational "touch points" that make you "talkable" will create accidental ambassadors for the "Brand Called You." So begin your storytelling adventure and have fun perfecting your "Art of Storytelling." Go beyond "fine" or "adequate" with a ho-hum beginning, middle and end. Instead, make yours a stimulating beginning, an engaging middle, and a provocative ending.

A few tips on how to test your storytelling capabilities. When using the word "story" as a preface, be aware of the reaction of your audience. Read their body language as your story unfolds. Are they following? Does a furrowed brow appear? Do they appear captivated or are their eyes wandering? If so try and rein them in... maybe you missed a key point...(middle before the beginning) or inject more enthusiasm into your narrative.

A second tip: ask for feedback by quite simply posing the question...did you get or follow my story? An interesting test is to hear when your story is repeated by others. What was retained and passed along? Don't think of your storytelling adventure as taking place in a structured environment with a feedback form, analysis and evaluation. It takes place in passing conversations, around the water cooler, or talking to your neighbor. The point is to become aware of the power of effective storytelling.

Third, LISTEN...become more aware of how others tell their stories. What do you remember as the captivating points or GEMS and why? Was is the way the story was told with enthusiasm and engaging eye contact? Perhaps it was the content that was woven in a plot, or conflict, or the manner of resolution that built momentum and ensured you were not disappointed at the end. What delighted you, made it memorable, or made it stick? In Part V you will see how your stories play out in a written context incorporating the GEMS. Here you will find examples of stories that integrate quotes, analogies, humor, childhood memories, references to heroes, mentors, favorite authors, musicians and idols. These BIO "GEMS" or excerpts are cited to help spark ideas for your narratives.

How to progress in perfecting your "Art of Storytelling?" It takes practice, feedback and listening to others. When you preface what you are about to say with the word "story," dropping that magical word into your lead sentence, you are setting expectations. Remember, there is even neurological evidence that points to the power of storytelling. Whether your audience is a friend, colleague, headhunter, child, client, prospect, or recruiter, you have set the stage with that five-letter word. You do not want to disappoint.

Storytelling Inspiring Questions

It's storytelling time! Following is a list of 35 questions that will help prompt the stories...get the juices flowing. Don't consider this an EXERCISE; that sounds too structured and formal. Play with the questions. I suggest you print out the list and carry it around with you. Take it out when you have a minute, a lull in the day, need a break, want to de-stress. Jot down notes in a haphazard way.

Is this a precise methodology? Not really. You could call it an approach, process, technique, way, path or procedure. In fact, there are no rules, time frame or criteria. The idea is to have fun...let your mind drift and let the stories surface. As you will see from the list, prompted stories can be personal or professional, from your childhood or adult life. Write what comes to mind immediately after you read the questions. Do It Yourself (DIY) or select questions to ask of a colleague, friend, coach, or child.

A child? Yes...that can be the true litmus test of your storytelling expertise. If you are an aunt, uncle, mother, father, brother, or sister...test your storytelling technique on a child. Why??? You will be forced to make your stories simple and easy to understand as your audience will have heightened expectations. Motivated to make your stories as captivating and amusing as possible, you will probably inject more energy, drama and enthusiasm. Go beyond just having a beginning, middle, and end...make it a stimulating beginning, an engaging middle, and a provocative ending that will leave your young listeners wanting more (note: adults will like it too). If you can tell a captivating story to a child around how you raised profits and successfully orchestrated an M & A in the middle of the financial crisis then you are a STAR! Try it!

So tell me a story...

1. About the funniest experience you ever had.
2. Where you developed, created, designed or invented something.
3. Accomplished more with the same or fewer resources.
4. About a practical joke you played that succeeded.
5. When you were given a project and you did more than expected i.e.,110% versus 100%.
6. About your bravest or most courageous moment.
7. Where you received an award or special recognition.
8. About the most harrowing experience you've ever had.
9. About the most impulsive thing you've ever done.
10. Where you saved the company a substantial amount of money.
11. About the story you never tired of hearing from your mom or dad.
12. When you were unexpectedly left "carrying the ball" and you jumped to the plate.
13. About how you increased sales.
14. Where you identified problems others did not see.

15. About your hero.

16. About when you were promoted or upgraded.

17. About your favorite childhood story.

18. Where you developed or implemented a new system or procedure.

19. Where you met company standards under unusual and difficult circumstances.

20. Where you handled effectively a crisis situation (professional or personal).

21. About the most influential person you've met.

22. About an experience where you accomplished the seemingly impossible.

23. About an encounter with a well-known individual that made a huge impression.

24. Where you did something where you really had to laugh at yourself.

25. When you were the most ill you've ever been.

26. About the most trying experience of your life.

27. About an experience in a foreign country that was a revelation of cultural differences.

28. About the worst injury you've ever sustained.

29. About the one moment or highlight in high school you'll never forget.

30. About competitions in which you excelled.

31. Where you worked successfully and completed a project with a stellar team.

32. Where you demonstrated individual drive and determination.

33. Where you juggled many projects simultaneously under deadline pressure.

34. About the one event in your childhood that had the greatest effect on your life.

35. About the one "lesson from mom" that you still live by today.

Emotional Intelligence (EQ) Stories

Findings based on the analysis of what competencies make people successful in jobs and organizations indicate that your Intelligence Quotient (IQ), indicating hard skills, takes second position to your Emotional Intelligence (EQ), indicating soft skills, in determining outstanding job performance. For this reason recruiters are scrutinizing candidates through this lens and probing more directed questions to make the EQ stories surface. In crafting your accomplishment stories (tool given in Part II) think in terms of the EQ skills in which you excel and have related stories. Use the circle that follows to visually segment and weight the four areas indicated below where you feel you are strong. These are the EQ constructs based on the Emotional Competencies (Goleman) model. Think of the stories that revolve around these areas and indicate your "proof of performance."

1. **Self-awareness**—the ability to read one's emotions and recognize their impact while using gut feelings to guide decisions.

2. **Self-management**—controlling one's emotions and impulses and adapting to changing circumstances.

3. **Social awareness**—the ability to sense, understand, and react to others' emotions while comprehending social networks.

4. **Relationship management**—the ability to inspire, influence, and develop others while managing conflict.

Interview with an Expert

Erin Yoshimura is Chief Empowerment Officer and Founder of Empowerful Changes.

Read her BIO at http://www.visibilitybranding.com or on her site at http://www.empowerful.com.

Q: Erin, as the EQ expert, can you first give me the one-liner on what is EQ?

A: To quote Daniel Goleman, PhD, who is credited for bringing EQ to the mainstream population, "Emotional intelligence is about saying the right thing to the right person at the right time with the right intensity." And, to add my take, if you find that you missed the mark on this, emotional intelligence is about having the courage to "stay in the room," both physically and emotionally, and the ability to continue the conversation that follows.

Q: How can EQ skills be woven into the storytelling of a Personal Brand?

A: Just as storytelling engages both the logical and emotional parts of the brain, EQ is about using both the logical and emotional sides of the brain to make better decisions and create optimal relationships. You need a good balance of both to be effective and compelling.

A large part of EQ is having deep awareness of emotions, yours and others, and utilizing that awareness to cultivate positive relationships. Stories provide more insight into your strengths and experience than just listing off your years of experience and education. Stories let people experience relating with you. That's what personal branding is all about.

EQ skills that you can weave into your personal brand story in order to make it authentic and relevant communicate an accurate self-assessment of empathy, transparency, "telling on yourself," how you handled conflict, what you achieved and how you impacted others.

In his book *A Whole New Mind*, Daniel Pink wrote, "The essence of persuasion, communication and self-understanding has become the ability to fashion a compelling narrative. When facts become so widely available and instantly accessible, each one becomes less valuable. What begins to matter more is the ability to place these facts in context and to deliver them with emotional impact."

Q: Can you give an example of effective storytelling around EQ skills?

A: I'll share one of my own stories although it begins with an example of a lack of EQ skills and not knowing my personal brand.

A while ago, I interviewed for an Executive Director's position with a social justice organization. Although I was interviewing in front of eight people simultaneously, I felt pretty confident in my answers. Then came the question that changed the entire outcome of the interview.

"Erin, what kind of manager were you?" I replied without hesitation, "I probably sucked as a manager," and continued to list several ways that I could have been better as a manager. This wasn't the answer they expected and it certainly wasn't one that I wanted to give. The unexpected question triggered my Asian cultural values of humility and modesty and resulted in my wiping out my past wins and achievements and the value I brought as a manager.

Had I known more about EQ and personal branding, I would have been equipped with many work experience stories that highlighted the challenges I faced as a manager, the actions I took and the end results I achieved. And, while there was always room for improvement, there were so many things that I did right as a manager.

Q: Are there any tools or assessments that you would recommend to discover (or as a basis for developing) EQ skills?

A: There are many tools available to assess EQ skills. For the individual contributor, I recommend http://www.talentsmart.com and taking the Emotional Intelligence Appraisal. It's a low-cost self appraisal ($40 USD) that also provides the client with six months of online EQ skill building. I particularly like this appraisal because it's more accessible and affordable to a diverse socio-economic group of people. For more resources on EQ, you can visit my website at http://www.empowerful.com.

Q: The messaging of EQ "stories" seems to be more and more important for individuals in career transition. Can you comment on this?

A: The stories we tell, whether positive or negative, hold vast amounts of insight into what's important to us and have emotional significance—if we delve deeper into them. By tapping into those stories, a person can uncover their vision, purpose, core values and passion and use that information to help them discover a new career path.

For me, the memories of countless times I didn't express my opinions and the feelings of being stuck in a job like a hamster on a wheel gave me a lot of insight into what's important to me, and in turn, informed my career decision. It's all about bringing one's dormant and subconscious passion to the surface and knowing that you can have a job you're passionate about. That's how a former techie turned into a trainer and coach.

Q: What's the difference between EQ and Personal Branding?

A: One of the reasons I'm so passionate about personal branding is because it's multipurpose in that it's a "must have" career management tool that empowers people to take charge of their careers while building emotional intelligence skills such as self-awareness, self-confidence, transparency, authenticity, innovation, influence and communication skills.

There's a lot of overlap between the two, but the main difference is that EQ is more focused on building powerful relationship and leadership skills by becoming acutely aware of your impact on others. EQ and personal branding work really well together in uncovering and cultivating the leader within each of us.

Leadership Storytelling

e all have been in leadership roles in some capacity, with or without an associated title. One student, a fresh MBA graduate, had no work experience. She lamented the fact that she had no career-related stories to tell about increasing profits, a stellar marketing campaign or launching a product. Through some probing around her leadership skills, it was discovered that during high school she was the captain of a dance and cheerleading squad of 30 high school girls. She organized weekly practices, schedules, logistics to transport the team to numerous in-state and out-of-state events and finally led them to championship status. That was impressive enough, but she also managed the gamut of personalities, from shy and timid to prima donna. And all this while scholastically maintaining a near 4.0 average. BINGO! She crafted a story using the Visibility Branding Storytelling Tool (VBST), found at the end of this section that clearly messaged her interpersonal and organizational skills to use in interviews. It was a great ice-breaker.

There has been a deluge of books written about leadership, offering a host of definitions and categories. Six areas have been chosen below as defined by Karl Albrecht. The ultimate leader, if he or she existed, would be strong in all of them. Again use the pie chart that follows to visually segment and weight the six areas indicated below where you feel you are strong. Think of the stories that indicate your "proof of performance."

NOTE: Refer to your answers and thoughts around the 35 Inspiring Questions in Part II, page 24.

1. VISION and VALUES
   A good leader envisions what should ideally happen, understands what is really happening, and recognizes what needs to be done to make that vision become a reality. They are decisive and spot problems.

2. DIRECTION
   Leaders help people accomplish tasks necessary to turn this vision into a reality. They set goals, establish priorities and delegate responsibility.

3. PERSUASION
   Leaders have the ability to persuade others to see, understand and believe in their vision. This is called "enrolling" others. They communicate the big picture and are good at communicating one-to-one.

4. SUPPORT
   Leaders make sure everyone is equipped with the necessary resources to accomplish tasks. They encourage creativity.

5. DEVELOPMENT
   Leaders challenge team members to learn new skills and act as mentors or coaches.

6. APPRECIATION
   Leaders recognize that everyone, no matter how sophisticated, educated or mature, wants respect and recognition. Good leaders respect the ideas and opinions of others and use ritual, celebration and ceremony to celebrate successes.

Personal Social Responsibility (PSR) Stories

rganizations have Corporate Social Responsibility (CSR) initiatives and stories stemming from sponsorship and cause-related campaigns, and so do personal brands. The term Personal Social Responsibility (PSR) refers to situations in which time or financial support for social, environmental or cultural concerns has been "gifted." Often, an individual's PSR is channeled where their vision, passion, values and interests lie. In the resume, this is often lost and may only be messaged in a few words or a line appearing at the bottom. For example, read Pierre Blanc's case story in Part III. Passionate about microfinance and with a history of volunteer activities, he wanted to transition from hi-tech, where his experience lay. His resume did not reflect his intended direction nor did it showcase his PSR initiatives and thought leadership on the subject. Pierre created an online portfolio that reflected his true personal brand. And the rest of the story...he found his dream position in microfinance, managing a team in Ghana. Read Pierre's story at http://www.pierreblanc.org.

There are many ways to start, build or develop PSR initiatives that align with your personal brand and values. Online you can "gift" your time without leaving home! This can take the form of offering mentoring, coaching, teaching or language tutoring. Whatever your skill set, there is a need. There are also many excellent causes you can support financially. Choosing one that corresponds with your values, interests and passions will only strengthen your brand. My personal favorite is Kiva, where for a minimum of $25, you can choose an entrepreneur in a developing country and help them to obtain small loans to launch their business. "Stories" about various entrepreneurs and their particular endeavors can be read on the Kiva site http://www.kiva.org. Read more about Kiva on page 151 as partial proceeds from the purchase of this book go towards financing Kiva entrepreneurs. Two other key PSR sites are: Ashoka http://www.ashoka.org and MercyCorps http://www.mercycorps.org.

KIVA
loans that change lives

Story Building around Assessment Results

ssessments are a great way to extract and identify key findings about the "Brand Called You" and then build the stories that exemplify the findings. More than ten assessments are identified, where experts are interviewed who shed light on how to incorporate assessment results into your story. Highlighted are the Myers Brigg (MBTI®), 360°Reach, Strength Finder and the Emotional Intelligence (EQ) Appraisal. These assessments can be used to identify and discover your EQ/IQ, leadership skills, key strengths and attributes.

Interview with an Expert

Susan Guarneri is the Career Assessment Goddess who has assisted thousands of professionals and executives with career transitions and job changes.

Read her BIO at http://www.visibilitybranding.com or on her site at http://www.AssessmentGoddess.com.

Q: As the Career Assessment Goddess, what categories of assessments lend themselves to developing content for storytelling and narratives?

A: The content for your stories and narratives center on your skills, strengths, interests, values, emotional intelligence, work style, leadership skills, and/or personal brand depending on the message you want to communicate and the target audience you are trying to reach. Fortunately, there are many reputable career assessments in all of these categories.

Q: As EQ and leadership skills are so important, which assessments can identify these skills?

A: There are two main groupings of assessments: self-assessments which you take yourself, and 360° feedback assessments which obtain the input of others. Ideally, regarding EQ and leadership, you would like to see the results from both camps for comparison purposes. If you happen to have a blind spot regarding a critical leadership skill, it would be imperative to get confidential feedback from respondents who are guaranteed anonymity.

Here are five EQ and Leadership assessments that provide for both self-assessment and feedback from external sources:

1. The 360°Reach Personal Branding Assessment incorporates the comparison feature and examines your leadership style, as well as your skills, strengths, weaknesses and personal attributes. All of these elements contribute to your emotional intelligence. Author Note: the 360° Assessment is covered in more detail later in this section. (http://www.reachpersonalbranding.com)

2. The Emotional Intelligence Appraisal™ Multi-Rater Edition provides a comparison of self-perception vs. what others see. The anonymous feedback comes via an online report with responses to open-ended questions. (http://www.talentsmart.com/products/surveys_flash.php?ID=44)

3. Leadership Report Using FIRO-B® and MBTI®is a self-assessment and explores leadership style in action and suggests how others in the organization may perceive and react to it. (http://www.cpp.com)

4. Co-authored by Ken Blanchard, the Preferred Leader Assessment measures the core leadership behaviors that earn the commitment and support of employees. (http://www.talentsmart.com/products/surveys.php?ID=27)

5. The 360° Refined™ Measures a leader's skill in the 22 Core and Adaptive leadership competencies most critical for job performance. Leaders rate themselves and receive ratings from their peers, supervisor(s), subordinates and others, such as customers.

The following self-assessments are useful for uncovering information about your skills, strengths, interests, preferred work environment, personal style and values. All of these are potential candidates for a juicy story supporting your personal brand!

1. The Strong Interest Inventory® and Myers-Briggs Type Indicator® Career Report (http://www.cpp.com) suggests work tasks that would be satisfying and work environments and career fields that would be a good fit. The report also includes ways to alter your work environment to make it more satisfying.

2. The Work Behavior Inventory Assessment suggests work style, leadership style, influencing/selling style, personality characteristics, emotional intelligence and indicators for occupational success.

3. The FIRO-B (The Fundamental Interpersonal Relations Orientation - Behavior) helps you to understand your own behavior and that of others in your interpersonal situations.

4. The MBTI Communications Style Report reveals your preferred communications style and how you can adapt it to better communicate with others.

5. The Values in Action (VIA) Survey of Character Strengths by Dr. Martin Seligman
(http://www.authentichappiness.sas.upenn.edu/Default.aspx)

6. The Brief Strengths Test by Dr. Martin Seligman
(http://www.authentichappiness.sas.upenn.edu/Default.aspx)

Q: How can the information from these assessments be woven into a brand message or story?

A: Your brand message needs to be relevant and compelling to your target audience AND be representative of the core theme of your brand. The results from your self-assessments and 360° feedback assessments can serve to consolidate your thinking about WHAT you have to offer that your target audience VALUES. This core theme and accompanying 3-5 strengths and values could be illustrated with stories from diverse aspects of your business, professional and personal life.

Q: Do you have an example of this with one of your clients?

A: One of my clients was an IT Project Manager who excelled at getting projects in on time or even ahead of schedule while holding down costs. This is something most employers would value. His brand story described how he got those results on a project he had inherited that had previously spiraled out of control. Through his persuasive communication skills and spirit of collaboration, he was able to build bridges and get cross-functional teams and external stakeholders to actually talk to one another productively! This client got the information for his brand story by evaluating and consolidating his results from the 360°Reach personal branding assessment and the MBTI Communications Style Report.

Q: Where can people go to learn more about career assessments?

A: You can learn more at my Career Assessment Goddess website (http://www.assessmentgoddess.com), including the article 'Looking for That Dream Job?' (http://www.assessmentgoddess.com/lookingforadreamjob.html), and explore the different types of career assessments and the benefits. In addition, check out my Career Goddess Blog for more practical advice and resources related to career assessments, job search, personal branding etc.

Interview with an Expert

Rebecca Castleton is a coach, consultant and the founder of Castleton Associates. A certified Myers-Briggs Type Indicator (MBTI) practitioner, she has used the MBTI with hundreds of individuals, teams and corporations.

Read her BIO at http://www.visibilitybranding.com or on her site at http://www.castletonassociates.com.

Q: To start...can you give us the short story on the MBTI?

A: Based on the psychological theories of Carl Jung—the famous Swiss psychoanalyst in the 1920's—the MBTI is a psychometric questionnaire designed to measure differences in how people perceive the world and make decisions. Later developed as an assessment by a mother-daughter team—Myers and Briggs—during the Second World War, the instrument was tested for over 40 years before it was accepted by the Educational Testing Service. Deemed the "most popular and valid instrument of its kind in the world," several million MBTI assessments are administered annually across the globe. The assessment focuses on normal populations and emphasizes the value of understanding naturally occurring differences.

Q: How does the MBTI offer an opportunity for personal brand exploration and how can it be used in creating a story based on specific job experiences and strengths and used in a job interview, BIO, or personal story?

A: By establishing individual preferences, the MBTI makes psychological types easy to understand and accept in everyday life. The premise is that as we begin to understand and accept our own behaviors, we will more easily understand and accept the differences of others we work with, live with, and love. Through a framework created by the instrument, the MBTI opens up possibilities for growth and development for each person. And through the process of validation with a certified Myers-Briggs practitioner, individuals can identify a personal path to excellence, with all preferences considered equally valuable.

Q: Do you have a story about how MBTI insights and results were used to weave a story?

A: David joined the police force in his thirties and was part of a group of twelve recruits. Over the years he found satisfaction in the work, but he also felt different from the others and he knew something was missing. An MBTI professional came to work with his group as a team-building exercise; each individual was administered the MBTI and went through a personal validation session. David realized through this work that he was "different" from the others, and began to recognize his strengths in leadership and strategy and his action-oriented approach, qualities that were not as evident in other team members. He worked with the consultant to develop a story—detailing how he had used these skills in his experiences with the team. He presented the story during his job evaluation and cited examples of how his leadership skills, visioning and strategy had moved the team forward. As a result, David became the team leader and was easily accepted by his other team members and quickly acknowledged for his strengths.

The 360°Reach Assessment

the first and leading personal brand assessment

The 360°Reach Assessment tool is in a category by itself. Why? Because it is the first and leading Web-based personal brand assessment that helps you get the real story about how you are perceived by those around you. It gives you the critical feedback you need to expand your career or business success. I use the 360°Reach as an integral part of the personal branding process and an indispensable tool for thriving in today's professional environment. Whether you are a job seeker, consultant or entrepreneur, the 360°Reach will provide you with the actionable insights you need to succeed.

Here is the 360°Reach in a nutshell with a few FAQ questions extracted from the Reach site. It is strongly recommended at a minimum to take the 15-day free trial. Better yet, purchase the paid version for 45 days; it gives you a 20-page report where your key skills and attributes are identified and will provide excellent content for crafting your accomplishment stories. The report also provides quotes from your respondents to incorporate into your messaging. (http://www.reachcc.com)

What is 360°Reach?

360°Reach is a personal brand assessment that provides you with the external insights that are essential to success. Developed by behavioral psychologists and branding experts, it gives you a focused portrait of your professional reputation—one that is invaluable for ongoing professional and personal development.

Who is 360°Reach for?

If you fall into any of the categories below, you can benefit tremendously from a 360°Reach Assessment:

- Career-minded professionals who want to develop professionally
- Individuals looking to change jobs
- Executives who need to understand how they are really perceived externally
- Independent consultants, entrepreneurs and small business owners who need external feedback to help guide their businesses
- Sales people and consultants who want to increase their visibility, presence, and effectiveness
- People who want to develop themselves personally and professionally
- Teams of people working inside companies

What kind of feedback does it provide?

360°Reach enables those people you select (respondents) to provide input about your rational and emotional attributes, your greatest strength and greatest weakness, the team role that most suits you, etc. It also provides your respondents with the opportunity to provide any additional comments they want to share.

References

eferences are one of the three essential elements in your Personal Brand Toolkit, along with your resume and BIO. The recognition you receive from others is tremendously valuable, as it provides a third-party assessment of your skills and abilities. Research shows recruiters now go beyond the traditional resume and expect endorsements of a candidate's brand from external sources. Make sure they find some GEMS that are relevant and compelling about yours.

Recommendations and testimonials also provide you with excellent excerpts and quotes to weave into your BIO content and can also be referenced in an interview situation, used as a lead-in to a good story. If for public view, such as your blog or website, be sure you have the writer's permission to use them. Requesting a recommendation gives you a good excuse to touch base with your key brand ambassadors and provide an update on your situation! You may already have references in your brand "toolkit" but if not, be proactive and use the KARMA strategy meaning GIVE or GIFT FIRST by writing one first for your contacts. This can easily be done on LinkedIn.

Third-party stories about your brand from previous employers, partners, clients, subordinates, professors, and colleagues can boost your credibility. People are more likely to believe what other people say about a brand. Think of how you, friends or colleagues might scan reviews on the Internet, before making a product purchase. The same process applies with the "Brand Called You." Your target will actively search to find interesting, third-party information about your brand.

Good recommendations or testimonials are solid equity that convey specifics about your talents and uniqueness. The best ones are short, but reveal more than the fact that you are a "nice" person with whom it's easy to work. They concretely showcase your accomplishments. Let your requestee do the editorializing, but feel free to coach them about what to include in the facts. The following samples will guide you, but of course add anything you can to make them more personal and original.

Sample Recommendation Request:

Dear _____,

Hope all is well for you at _____. Here's an update on my situation: (give indication of what you are looking for). For this reason, I would greatly appreciate a letter of reference/recommendation. As I know you are busy and I value your time, I have provided below some key facts that you may want to include:

Date of your position or time frame of your relationship _____

Title during period referenced _____

Major highlights/accomplishments/projects (don't assume they remember what you did)

- _____

- _____

- _____

If you could write a brief recommendation by (DATE), I would be very pleased to return the favor now or in the future.

Regards,

_____

Sample Recommendation:

To Whom It May Concern,

It is my pleasure to recommend _____ for the position of _____.

I first met _____ in (DATE) where he/she (indicate relationship). In this capacity he/she worked on/accomplished/was responsible for _____.

Thanks to his/her efforts _____ (indicate actions/results). His/her ability to _____ was very impressive. As a capable, personable and energetic individual he/she would be a great asset to your organization.

Feel free to contact me for any further information.

Regards,

_____

Character References:

You may be asked to write a character reference for placement on LinkedIn or for other purposes. Again you might also employ KARMA-based GIVE or GIFT FIRST strategy of submitting one for a colleague before getting one back. The relationship in this case is not directly related to the work environment so the reference describes personal qualities and general skills.

Here is an example:

"Isabelle has a unique blend of professionalism, marketing knowledge, talent, and enthusiasm. Her marketing solutions for luxury hotels are highly creative and distinctive. In fact, the name she chose for her company, Unique Experiences, says it all: She meets and exceeds her clients' expectations."

LinkedIn Recommendations:

If you are on LinkedIn, then your profile most likely appears at the top of the search results. Want to verify? Google yourself by typing your name in quotation marks. If your LinkedIn profile is one of the first few results, this means recruiters, potential clients, investors and candidates will likely click on your profile to find out more about your brand. For this reason, LinkedIn is an excellent platform to not only showcase your recommendations but to write for others as well.

Rather than using the REQUEST A RECOMMENDATION feature on LinkedIn, use the Karma based GIVE or GIFT approach. Writing a recommendation for someone else first not only enriches your relationships, it almost always leads to one in return. LinkedIn even does the asking for you, automatically, when you write a recommendation.

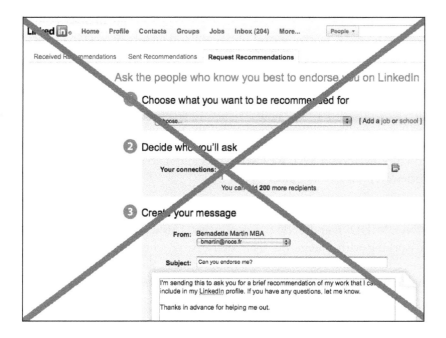

The Visibility Branding Storytelling Tool (VBST)

n PART II you have been given various ways to develop and extract stories around your EQ and leadership skills, volunteer activities, Personal Social Responsibility (PSR), assessment results and references. Now it's time to DISTILL 5-7 key stories, develop these in more detail and structure them, choosing the ones that will resonate most with your target. Mix personal and professional stories, using the VISIBILITY BRANDING STORYTELLING TOOL (VBST).

How will this tool help? Have you ever noticed when telling a story at a networking event or at an interview, you get a *blank stare* or *furrowed brow*? You sense the attention dissipating and see eyes wandering. In fact, it may be that your flow was jumbled and non-sequential. You were not relating elements or transitions key to making sense of the story from the listener's perspective. Using an accomplishment tool helps your stories flow, by incorporating these basic elements: SITUATION, CHALLENGE, ACTION, RESULTS and TESTIMONIALS. Working on accomplishment stories provides you with mini stories and excellent content to weave into your "Big Picture."

There are many formulae for structuring your stories. Some use the acronyms STAR, CAR and SMART. The VBST builds on the basic structure by adding KEY ATTRIBUTES and TESTIMONIALS to give stories even more resonance.

At the basic level, all accomplishment structures incorporate a BEGINNING, MIDDLE and END to your stories. This may seem obvious, but, in working with clients on their delivery, coaches (and interviewers) notice how frequently storytellers jump around. Sometimes the middle comes before the beginning, the end is disclosed before the stage is set, or pertinent facts are revealed out of order. This non-sequential relay is hard to follow; it forces the listener to retract, back up, remember, put the pieces in place and cobble the story together. This exertion of mental energy distracts from the story, dilutes it, lessens its impact and makes the listener focus on the flow rather than the content of your story.

Whether your target is the hiring decision-maker, prospect, or client, don't make him or her DIG for the stories. Tell them in a succinct and clear manner. The VBST gives you a structure and flow to use as a foundation for telling your stories. Your target wants to hear about specific accomplishments. Writing it down is well worth your time. Not only will you not have to dredge them up from memory when the time comes, you'll appear confident, professional, and poised.

Accomplishment Story #1 (goal is to develop 5-7 to have in your "back pocket")

SHORT TITLE: _____

THREE KEY WORDS: Cite only three key strengths, skills (EQ/IQ) or attributes that this accomplishment story highlights about you.

1. _____
2. _____
3. _____

DATE AND PLACE: _____

SITUATION: Set the stage; lay the foundation for the story. (e.g., in job transition, just got laid off, stock market collapsed...)

_____
_____
_____
_____
_____

CHALLENGE: Was there a conflict, need, difficulty, danger, or a protagonist (*e.g.*, deadline to meet, no resources, financial crisis...)

_____

_____

_____

_____

_____

ACTIONS: What steps did you take to solve the problem or get results? Use bullet points and action verbs. See page 136 for list of action verbs. (*e.g.*, organized a virtual team, convinced the Board of Directors, etc...)

_____

_____

_____

_____

_____

RESULTS: What was the end situation, outcome, resolution or transformation? Can you add quantifiable figures or measurable results to identify scale and scope? Use bullet points and action verbs. (*e.g.*, received a promotion, improved ROI, launched the first...)

_____

_____

_____

_____

_____

TESTIMONIALS: Here include any recognition, quotes, testimonials, press clippings, feedback, comments either verbal or written that you received either formally or informally. (*e.g.*, the press raved, it was on CNN, the client said....)

_____

_____

_____

_____

_____

It is one thing to present the tool but let's give an example (anonymity retained) of how this plays out in a concrete sense.

Carole's Story

TITLE: Global Corporate Legal Affairs Conference for Fortune 100 Company

DATE AND PLACE: Prague, October 2009

KEYWORDS: Time Management, Organized, Detail Oriented

SITUATION:
The Corporate HQ Board decided to organize a worldwide meeting, inviting 250 high level managers, coming from all continents. The initial person in charge of the meeting fell ill, and I was called at the "very last minute" to take over. All the bookings, arrangements, and programs were not ready. This was on top of my current responsibilities (including a major internal meeting for 250 marketing and sales employees in Martinique).

CHALLENGE:

- Sending and centralizing all the invitations within a very short framework

- Large scale and demanding audience: 250 CEOs, GMs, and politicians

- Tight time constraints: 15 days

- Paying attention to time-consuming details to maintain a high-quality work level

ACTIONS:

- Defined needs, sent out invitations and centralized logistics

- Negotiated with the hotel, travel agency, limousine service, local restaurants and guides

- Organized parallel group meetings and telephone conferences pre- and post-conference

- Prepared the compilation of the presentation on CD-ROM for participants to take home

- Organized appropriate sight-seeing activities for participants and partners

- Organized post-conference stays for participants

RESULTS:

The conference was a real success. As a consequence I was offered a job at the Belgian Headquarters in Public Relations.

TESTIMONIALS:

"In Prague, Carole really saved the European reputation by organizing a key strategic worldwide meeting."

"Carole's sense of organization, involvement and professionalism turned the meeting into a real success."

"Carole is the Queen of Worldwide Conferences."

"Carole's interpersonal skills and her incredible ability to take on board heavy workloads made the challenge possible!"

Part III: 2.0 Storytelling— Communicating Your Story Online

"Story is far older than the art of science and psychology, and will always be the elder in the equation no matter how much time passes."
Clarissa Pinkola Estes

DISCOVER * DEVELOP * DISTILL* DIGITIZE * DISSEMINATE * DISCLOSE * DOCUMENT * DESIGN

Storytelling 2.0. highlights interactive tools and the emerging technology available for telling and disseminating personal narratives on Google, Twitter, LinkedIn, YouTube, and in video storytelling and virtual worlds. Trends in this space are identified in a series of interviews with experts and thought leaders: an Online Video Branding Expert, a Google Goddess and SEO Sage and a Virtual World Virtuoso. Recruiters and Human Resource (HR) professionals share their thoughts on how they currently search for candidates with this "New Process," which could mean that the traditional resume is dead. Three online professional portfolio sites showcase how a corporate executive, an entrepreneur and a professional in career transition achieved the ultimate in managing their online identities.

- Storytelling 2.0 or Digital Storytelling
- Storytelling on Google

- Video Storytelling

- Storytelling in 3D Virtual Worlds

- Case Stories: Online Portfolio Examples

Storytelling 2.0 or Digital Storytelling

It is no longer around the fire, huddled after a day of bison hunting, that we tell our stories. Now, we can choose from countless affordable, sophisticated, and easy-to-use platforms to get our story out to the world. The implications of Web 2.0 and technological innovations on the way we interact, connect and communicate are staggering. With so many technology-mediated experiences, so many ways to connect with our target and build a relationship across media, it can be overwhelming. At another level it can be an opportunity. However, getting people to listen to your stories, *aha*...now that's another matter. These powerful communication tools, a veritable social media "hub" of choices, can be daunting. Facebook, LinkedIn, Twitter, YouTube, Second Life, virtual worlds, blogs...we need to find and select with INTENTION and a STRATEGY the channels of digital storytelling media that you can relate to and more important, relate to your target.

PART III isn't about advising you on where and how you should be telling your story in the digital realm. Instead, this Part leads you through a series of interviews with experts in the field of digital storytelling and presents perspectives and insights on trends, interactive tools, social media and virtual worlds. Interviewed are Julie Vetter the Google "Goddess"; Lou Bortone, the Online Branding Video Guy; and Serge Soudoplatoff, Virtual World Expert.

Also, recruiters and Human Resource professionals share their thoughts on how they find, select, and evaluate candidates based on their online presence...the "New Process" of selecting candidates. Maybe the resume is dead! The plethora of digital and 2.0 ways to tell our story can however dilute your brand. In constructing your identity in various media and venues these identities should share core elements and not vary schizophrenically from medium to medium. The HR professionals quoted have cumulative experience interviewing hundreds of candidates and reviewing hundreds of resumes. They shed some light on where they find "the story" on a candidate and they all agree that the traditional resume and interview is no longer the primary source.

Although your story is ever morphing, re-purposed and adapted to the context or situational relevance at hand, it should nevertheless remain clear and consistent across all mediated experiences. Online storytelling has clear implications for personal and professional advancement in building your career or business; the value and impact is huge. This doesn't mean manipulating the facts and creating "spin" or portraying a drastically different persona on one social media platform versus another. It means being authentic—appreciating and becoming aware of what you have to offer, understanding how it relates to the needs of your target and finding the most effective way to communicate your potential.

Updates and trends in new technology can be found on the respective experts' websites. Bookmark their sites, add to your RSS feed and sign up for their newsletters.

Storytelling on Google

Interview with an Expert

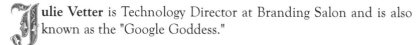

Julie Vetter is Technology Director at Branding Salon and is also known as the "Google Goddess."

Read her BIO at http://visibilitybranding.com or on her site at http://www.julievetter.com.

Q: What is the impact of Google in telling our online story?

A: Google's mission is "to organize the world's information and make it universally accessible and useful." Google has more than 64% of the search market. Google is the most recognized brand in the world, according to a recent article in the *San Francisco Chronicle*.

Google's purpose applies to information in whatever form arises on the Internet, from text to video to chat, even reaching into your phone with Google Voice. In order to tell your story on the Web showing up in Google search results for your name or service is one of the top priorities—especially for job seekers—with the classic "Googling" your name by potential employers as their first recourse to finding out more about you. Facebook is now also checked by 30% of potential employers.

Q: This book includes current ways of job searching and finding candidates. What are the more innovative trends you have seen or predict?

A: Murphy-Goode winery ran a terrific job search in 2009. They posted an announcement on their website asking for people interested in running their online marketing to submit a video of themselves, explaining why they were the best choice. The videos were public and anyone could watch and submit a vote for their favorite candidate. There was a huge response from across the country. Submission of video introductions of job seekers will become more and more common.

Sites such as LinkedIn, which answers the question "How to get in touch with so-and-so?," alumni associations, businesses and networks will offer more and more applications for use with smart phones. Connecting with others through an application that tells you which participants at a job fair, for example attended the same school, have the same skill set, belong to the same groups and even where they are physically located in relation to you.

Q: As covered in this book there are so many opportunities to tell your story across so many media. How will all this information be managed?

A: The response to this social media splitting of our online identities has been the rise of aggregators, tools that bring all these disparate parts back together again. Note that some of these providers may have disappeared by the time you read this book, but others will arise wherever the need is.

Try searching for "Julia Child" on http://addictomatic.com/ and you will see all the references to her across all media from videos to tweets to Google news to WordPress blog posts.

Lijit is a personal search engine that will give results for content you have posted to your social accounts, helping your audience (and you!) find useful information you have shared.

Another new area that is just starting to expand is about establishing your reputation virtually. http://www.thewhuffiebank.org—*The Whuffie Bank* is a nonprofit organization dedicated to building a new currency based on reputation that could be redeemed for real and virtual products and services. The higher your reputation, the wealthier you are.

Q: I have noticed that many associations and groups that are going online are using Facebook and are morphing their sites into FB as the platform of preference instead of creating their own. Can you comment on this?

A: Facebook is growing at a tremendous pace—there are more users than the population of the United States as of September, 2009. But there are inherent challenges with attempting to serve so many people and for most people the interface does not make it easy enough to implement proper privacy settings. Security is a big problem that Facebook has to deal with responsibly and successfully.

Facebook is trying to provide divisions for people, commercial interests and groups by establishing separate profiles and pages. The downside of Facebook is that it tries to do so much. I think LinkedIn will remain a priority for professionals wanting to connect for business purposes because it focuses on doing that, as long as it keeps improving upon that mission.

Q: What about Twitter? Seems that after FB, Twitter is the new kid on the block that has experienced explosive growth. How does Twitter factor currently in the way we tell our story and create a presence?

A: Twitter filled a specific need and hit on a very precise form of communication—one sentence—that gave them the lead in a new domain. It is a phenomenon for viral marketing. For branding oneself it also has interesting applications. There is a man with a crème brûlée cart in San Francisco whose business boomed when he started tweeting his daily location and menu. If you are creative and like reading and sending one-sentence sound bytes of information that will become a part of your virtual identity.

Q: What are the measurement tools you have seen emerge that measure your online identity and reputation?

A: The aforementioned aggregators tell you where you are being seen. Google news alerts are a great way to create a free press clipping service for yourself. Test your online visibility regularly with this tool from Career Distinction: "What's Your Google Quotient" at http://www.careerdistinction.com/onlineid/

Once you have done the work to clarify your own story, use the tools to express it that are common to those in your sector, plus the social media services that you find engaging. Posting your story on Facebook and never going back, setting up a Twitter account and never tweeting will become a part of your online identity.

"My advice for professionals regarding Facebook. You need to be aware that some recruiters will see it, so either keep it private or just check on whether it's projecting the image you want a potential employer or headhunter to have. I don't mean that you need to censor everything but perhaps think about the photo you use or not putting up "XXX hates his/her job" at 2.20 pm in the afternoon! I don't use Facebook for professional reasons but some people do. Recently, a friend looking for someone to fill a position had interviewed a number of people, then checked them out on FB and lost confidence in every single one!"
- Annalisa Riches, Senior European HR Business Partner at Sabre and lastminute.com

Video Storytelling

Interview with an Expert

ou **Bortone** is Founder and Creative Director of Online Video Branding, LLC.

Read his BIO at http://www.visibilitybranding.com or on his site http://www.OnlineVideoBranding.com.

Q: How can video capture a person's story?

A: Video has long been the best medium to capture a person's story, whether it's in a 30-second television commercial or a half-hour long documentary. In our visually-oriented society, there is simply no more compelling method of storytelling than through video. Video is immediate, personal and captivating.

The difference today is that video can capture *anyone's* story. Before the Internet and the "Online Video Revolution," the power of video was controlled by the media elite. A handful of major television networks and media conglomerates essentially determined *whose* story would be told. You had to wait for the media to come to you.

Today, that power has shifted to the individual. Anyone with an Internet connection and a webcam can tell their own story on video, and broadcast it via the Web instantly to millions of people worldwide. YouTube and other video sites are media for the masses. (YouTube has also quickly emerged as the fourth most visited website on the Internet and the second most popular search engine, right behind Google!)

Now, rather than having the media moguls decide who we see on video, the public decides by watching and sharing videos via YouTube and social media. The entire media landscape has shifted, and everyone who has access to the Internet now has access to the storytelling capabilities of video.

Q: What do you see as the trends in video use as a storytelling resource?

A: As online video becomes even more mainstream and easier to access, more people will continue to adopt Web video as a messaging and communication tool. Not only will video become a communications tool used daily—such as the telephone or email—but video as a marketing tool will also become more popular. The public will make or break new video "stars" almost overnight by sharing videos and making a video go "viral."

Traditional businesses and major brands will attempt to capitalize on this trend, only to find that viral video can't be manipulated or manufactured. "Mass media" will now be determined by the media masses! Creativity and originality will rule the day. Online video will create an opportunity for the "little guy" to tell his or her story every bit as powerfully as the media titans. The playing field has been leveled....

Q: How will people be telling their story in 2015 and beyond?

A: We've already got "social media mania" today and that will continue to flourish. Webcams, Web-conferencing and even iPhone video conversations will be an everyday occurrence. We will basically be able to see and interact with each other anytime, anywhere, with as much transparency and immediacy as we want.

The comic book fiction of "Dick Tracy communicator watches" will become reality, with new communications gadgets that take cell phones to the next level. One downside of this "always on" communication may be our lack of privacy. If an iPhone can tell me exactly where you are at any given moment, you can imagine what that technology will be able to do five or ten years from now! Video email and video phone calls will be as common as regular email or instant messaging.

With all this access to instant communication, it will not be so much how we tell our story with video, but how we conduct our business in general over time. In other words, we may not be judged by a particular video, as much as our reputation will be determined by our online behavior or our cumulative video history. If our lives are more of an "open book," then the story is who we are all the time, not just when we're sending a video or delivering one, particular message. It won't be enough to just tell a story, we have to live the story....

Q: How does video branding factor into Storytelling 2.0?

A: Transparency will be the watchword of Storytelling 2.0. Video branding will be how we live the brand in public, because so much of our business will be "out in the open" for all to see. "Brand You" will not be in sound bites or video clips, but in how you conduct your overall business and manage your reputation.

This is good news for those of us who don't mind the spotlight and who have nothing to hide. With video so pervasive, it will be much more difficult to "manufacture" an image or brand. Fortunately, if you live your values and do business with integrity, the "story" will tell itself.

Q: Can you cite some creative uses of video to message a story?

A: Perhaps the most recent example is that of Barack Obama's Presidential campaign. The campaign embraced social media and online video, and was probably the most open and transparent campaign in US history. It was such a compelling story, all they had to do was let it unfold on video—especially on the Internet, where the story was being told minute-by-minute, as it happened.

Q: Any additional observations and predictions?

A: I recently predicted that there would be a "gold rush" to grab TV domain names, just like there was a land grab for .com names. This is because everyone will have their own Web TV channel or video website, such as http://www.LouBortone.tv.

As we continue to create more of a video presence, we will need a dedicated website or "hub" for all our videos. "Dot TV" websites may serve that purpose. In addition, look for social media sites like Twitter and Facebook to become even more video-friendly, perhaps setting up a page or site just for video tweets, etc.

YouTube will also continue to grow, but may become more like traditional radio with "channels" or stations. In other words, there will be so many videos on YouTube, that they will have to create sub-channels, *e.g.*, YouTube Business, YouTube Comedy, YouTube How-To, or YouTube Music. This will create new opportunities for even more niche-specific video messaging.

Online video will become much more common, but the technology will be more and more user friendly. Creating and sending videos will be as quick and easy as shooting off an email. Content will be king and quality will be secondary.

Even now, there are new websites such as http://www.OneTrueMedia.com, http://www.JayCut.com, and http://www.Animoto.com that allow people to create fast, easy, professional and free videos for emailing or posting online. This first generation of "instant video" websites will lead to new resources for making video even easier and less technical.

One final caveat: Storytelling is and always will be about the "story" first. Regardless of the technology, the story must be compelling. You must captivate your viewer. No technology is going to replace good old imagination and creativity!

In closing, the way I like to look at online video is this: If a picture is worth a thousand words, then a video must be worth a million!

Author's Note: There are many innovative ways to use video as an online communication tool that can be dropped into your email signature, website, newsletter, blog or even posted on professional networks. Video can be used by job seekers, entrepreneurs, executives and employees looking to educate, share a point of view or promote their business or personal brand. It is a compelling way to create connections with people and bring personality into your communication mix. There are DIY (Do-It-Yourself) resources that include:

- http://www.OnlineVideoBranding.com
- http://www.webvideouniversity.com
- http://www.personalbranding.tv

If you are a professional then you want to look professional. As with your professional photograph, if you are incorporating video into your communication mix you may want to consider using professional services. Here is an example of a professionally shot video of a colleague Paul Copcutt as produced by http://www.VideoBIO.com.

http://www.videoBIO.com/paulcopcutt

Another example of using video is EuroBusiness Media (EBM), the European leader in providing online CEO interviews to the global investment community. Run by an experienced team of financial television journalists, they have helped to establish management interviews as a best practice for effective financial communications. EBM's main product is 'CEO-DIRECT,' a Web-based distribution network which broadcasts streaming video interviews of CEOs directly by email to investors, analysts, traders and brokers worldwide. Here is Maurice Lévy, CEO, Publicis Groupe.

Video link http://www.eurobusinessmedia.com/interview-Flash.php?id_article=509

Storytelling in 3D Virtual Worlds

Interview with an Expert

erge Soudoplatoff, Founder of HYPERDOXE, http://www.hyperdoxe.net, is a thought leader on virtual worlds.

Read his BIO at http://www.visibilitybranding.com or on his blog: http://www.hyperdoxe.net

Q: Companies and individuals are telling their stories in virtual worlds. To start, could you enlighten readers on what is a virtual world and give some examples?

A: A **virtual world** is an online community in a computer-based simulated environment. Users take the form of avatars and can inhabit and interact with one another and use and create objects. An **avatar** is a computer user's representation of himself/herself or an alter ego, usually in the form of a two or three-dimensional model. Examples of virtual worlds are Second Life, World of Warcraft, Everquest, Disney's Club Penguin, and Mattel's BarbieGirls.com, to name a few.

Q: How are companies telling their story in 3D virtual worlds?

A: Linden Labs, creator of the virtual world Second Life and IBM have developed enterprise solutions for security-rich, custom virtual world creation and collaboration on the Second Life Grid platform that is behind IBM's firewall. This allows dynamic content creation tools and a vibrant user community. The goal is to create a solution that businesses can quickly deploy to interact and get work done in a new way.

Q: With the growth in virtual jobs...many people have never met their clients face-to-face except via webcam. Will 3D virtual worlds be the place of the future to interact with clients? What are the advantages and any disadvantages?

A: Virtual does not replace real, it just makes it more efficient. Go back before the Internet: when you meet a customer, you spend half an hour listening to the customer explaining who he is. Now, you surf on his website, and when you meet, you go straight forward to the purpose of the meeting. The time you spend with him is the same, but the quality of the interaction has improved. When it is about organizing meeting with many people, the gain in preparation time is even bigger with the Internet. Virtual worlds will make this gain even bigger. Preliminary feedback suggests that knowledge acquisition is better inside a virtual world.

Q: Which companies are considering or are already present in virtual worlds?

A: At a conference for businesses seeking to understand and maximize business strategies using virtual worlds the attendees were BP Group, Johnson and Johnson, Chevron, Ernst and Young, KPMG, Intel, Cisco, Gartner, Indiana University, Sun Microsystems and more. This gives you an idea of who the innovators and early adopter organizations are. Some companies have already conducted interviews inside virtual worlds. Accenture is an example. This took place in Second Life mostly in 2007 and 2008.

Q: Can you explain what you mean by saying that the Web is not where people truly interact? You mentioned there is no emotion. Can you explain? How is this different in virtual worlds?

A: When you surf on a website, you do not know who the other people are who are surfing on the same website at the same time. You could have friends, relatives, colleague, partners, etc... So, on the Web, you interact with content. On the opposite hand, tools like Webex allow you to interact on content, but there is no emotion. A virtual world is really the best tool to synchronously interact with other people on shared content, without the necessity to be physically in the same room.

Q: Are there jobs in virtual worlds and if so where?

A: Yes, there are jobs within and around virtual worlds. By the latter I mean that first of all, you need to build virtual worlds. So you need virtual architects and virtual landscapers, who create the geography. Then you need to put objects, so you need virtual designers who are able to create beautiful 3D objects. Then you need to dress your avatar properly, so you must find other virtual designers. Have a look at http://www.shenlei.wordpress.com for an example of someone who has created a fashion research institute in Second Life.

Once you have the objects, they must interact with avatars, or avatars with avatars. So you need to program, using a programming language. It is called "scripting" in Second Life or other virtual worlds platforms. Then, if you create a serious game as an example, you must write scenarios for learning. Then, in virtual worlds, you can buy land, and loan it. Or you can loan virtual money, etc. At http://www.acs.anshechung.com you will see the history of a lady who created a multi-million dollar company by first buying and renting land in Second Life, then by selling more sophisticated services in other virtual world platforms.

Case Stories: Online Portfolio Examples

The ultimate way to control your online identity is to create a professional online portfolio with your own visual identity and branding. This is the next step up for many whose online presence to date has been their LinkedIn profile. There are template-based services or you may want to work with a graphic designer and website developer where you will have more flexibility in terms of layout, design, applications, features and interactivity.

Case Story #1

Lynda Sydney: Entrepreneur

Lynda is a freelance advertising copywriter from Toronto, Canada. After gaining solid agency experience in both account management and creative, she began freelancing full-time in 2001. She's been working in both Paris and Toronto since 2005.

When potential clients would express interest in Lynda's services, her traditional resume did not convey the entire story of her unique and well-rounded background in marketing, communications and copywriting. She was on LinkedIn but she felt she needed a document that would showcase her skills and describe the services she provides in a concise and compelling way. She started with a tool that was a combination of her BIO and SERVICES that succinctly highlighted her unique background and skills, and detailed the services she offers.

Lynda Sydney
Advertising Copywriter

Thinking Strategically. Writing Creatively.

Lynda Sydney is an advertising copywriter from Toronto, Canada with over ten years of writing experience. Her solid agency background includes positions in both account management and creative. She has worked with clients in industries such as telecommunications, technology, financial services, romance publishing, media, education and household products.

The nature of her work is "have laptop, will travel" and with a passion for France and clients on both sides of the pond, she divides her time between Paris and Toronto. With her combined experience in marketing and writing, Lynda has a unique combination of skills that enable her to think strategically and write creatively.

Copywriting Services

With a background in the highly measurable area of direct mail, Lynda has moved into results-driven online media, working in search engine optimization (SEO) copywriting and Google Ads. She can provide copywriting services for strategic marketing and advertising projects, taking your product/service and message, and creating concise and compelling advertising copy. Her work includes:

Direct Mail	Sale Letters	Brochures	Newsletters
Sell Sheets	Websites	Web Promos	Banner Ads
Print Ads	Catalogue	Radio	Postcards
Self-mailers	Google Ads	E-zines	E-bulletins
Scripts for CDs/Online Demos		PowerPoint® Presentations	

Editing and Proofreading Services

For companies who want to expand their reach into the English language market, Lynda can also provide adaptation, proofreading and editing services. You spend much time and energy ensuring that your web site and other marketing materials present your image professionally in your native language. Lynda can help you present a professional image in English as well.

Contact Information

Lynda Sydney
Freelance Advertising Copywriter
lsydney@sympatico.ca
Toronto: +1 416.495.7215
Paris: +33 (0)6.27.68.15.32

Creating an online portfolio was an important next step in expanding her client base, allowing potential clients in different countries to view her work samples virtually.

After a process of searching for websites she liked and creating a light-box of images she felt were consistent with her personal brand, Lynda developed her Web presence by building an online portfolio. Her portfolio page lets clients click on the links to see PDF samples of print work, access websites, listen to radio spots or view commercial videos. To complete her online portfolio, Lynda included a narrative BIO, a services page, client testimonials and a page of links to related sites and services.

Since Lynda is passionate about driving, she designed http://www.CarChick.ca, a fun and informative blog for women who love to drive, delivered with Lynda's playfulness and sense of humor.

All these actions had great results. One of Lynda's contacts recently recommended her to a colleague who said Lynda had one of the best and most interesting BIOs she had ever read.

And since launching her blog, Lynda has been networking with women in the automotive industry. Upon viewing CarChick.ca, the owner of an automotive service centre for women in Western Canada said, "It's fabulous. I love what you're doing!"

Lynda has also incorporated her online portfolio and blog addresses into her email signature. When clients ask for more information, she simply sends them to her site or blog. In today's Web savvy world where everyone "Googles" practically everyone they meet, having a Web presence that she can include on her business card has given her added credibility as a dedicated business professional who "has laptop and will travel."

To read Lynda's full BIO visit http://www.lyndasydney.com. Check out her blog at http://www.CarChick.ca.

Lynda Sydney
Copywriter

Home
Services
Portfolio
Testimonials
About
Links I Like!
Contact

Email Lynda Sydney
Toronto: 416 485 7215
Paris: +33 (0)6 27 68 15 32

Thinking Strategically. Writing Creatively.

Lynda Sydney is a copywriter who provides writing services for strategic marketing and advertising projects in both traditional and online media. As a copywriter with experience in account management, she will work with you to understand your company's products, services, industry and target market, turning your message into concise and compelling copy.

With a solid background as a direct mail copywriter, and enjoying the highly measurable medium of direct mail, Lynda has moved naturally into results-driven online media, such as search engine optimization (SEO) copywriting and Google Ads.

Responsive, dependable and deadline driven, Lynda is a professional copywriter whose goal is to partner with her clients for their marketing success.

Case Story #2

Pierre Blanc: Professional in Career Transition

Pierre, a dynamic young business professional, worked at PricewaterhouseCoopers (PwC) as a Logistics Consultant for three years, and at IBM as a Marketing Manager for three years. In 2007, he spent four months trying to make a major career change from hi-tech to microfinance.

Despite the competencies he'd acquired, Pierre was not satisfied with the path that his professional life was taking. He'd spent nine years of his youth in a developing country and felt his true calling was to work where he could contribute to elevating people out of poverty. With this objective in mind, he had started a job search in the fields of fair trade and microfinance. But, after four months of looking, he had no solid leads.

Pierre realized his resume didn't reflect his intended career direction. He needed a strong summary statement to highlight his skills and his strong motivation to work in these new fields. An initial step was to add a "Summary of Qualifications" to his resume to message his crossover competencies that were in line with those required in his target fields. However, he went even further and designed a personal website. This allowed him to display his strong motivation and to showcase his volunteer efforts and initiatives in these fields which compensated for his lack of professional experience. In addition to increasing his visibility to his target and network, it increased his legitimacy, by showing the recruiter that he was knowledgeable.

These actions yielded three positive results. First, they clarified Pierre's personal brand, direction and aspirations. In his words: "I was more confident in selling myself." The second was to render him more visible and legitimate in the eyes of recruiters. Pierre did not have "paid" experience in the fields he targeted, but by bringing forward his strengths, volunteer activities, motivation and professional and personal paths, he stood out amidst more experienced candidates.

The rest of the story...the microfinance recruiter who hired Pierre told him the website contributed to his being chosen. Pierre feels that his optimized resume also played a significant part in giving him a shot at a new professional life! http://www.pierreblanc.org

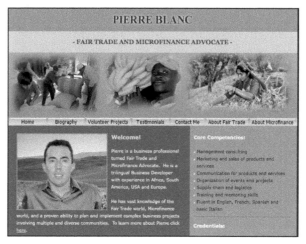

Case Story #3

Fabio Ferrari: Executive Online Portfolio

Like many professionals, Fabio wanted to take control of his online identity. As a forward thinking executive, he planned to create a personal website that messaged his vast experience, accomplishments, emotional intelligence and leadership skills. Fabio had a profile on LinkedIn, but he wanted to expand his visibility with his own visual branding and increase his Google ranking.

A major challenge was that he shared his name with a filmmaker, a model, and a race car driver. Fabio needed to be found easily, with clear and consistent messaging that reached the right audience.

To this end, he created a full online professional portfolio, taking a very visual approach. Various pages were designed to showcase his key achievements in the form of accomplishment stories. He included a short and longer narrative BIO, a reference page with photos and a page about his interests. With a mix of professional and candid photos, Fabio comes across as multi-dimensional, and alive. And, the ensemble makes an interesting and captivating story!

Fabio achieved excellent Google rankings. Now, when his name is Googled, his site appears at the top of the first page following by his LinkedIn profile, which has consistent information with his portfolio site.

Fabio has received positive feedback about the website from professional recruiters, colleagues and friends. http://www.fabioferrari.eu

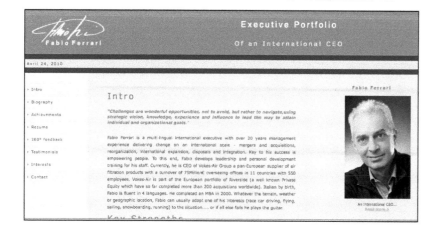

Part IV: Offline Storytelling

DISCOVER * DEVELOP * DISTILL* DIGITIZE * **DISSEMINATE** * **DISCLOSE** * DOCUMENT * DESIGN

Time to DISSEMINATE and DISCLOSE your goldmine of well-structured stories and to tell your "mini-stories" orally in interviews and the elevator pitch (your 60-second commercial) where you finesse your "story" into an effective one-liner. Also, refine your oral presentation, reduce verbal graffiti and critique yourself with a feedback form (or use with a colleague). Your personal image and appearance have a great impact, so a stellar image consultant offers advice on enhancing your visual impression. Discover top interview questions that can lead into the stories you have developed. Read what Human Resource professionals and recruiters say about storytelling in the interview.

- Interview Storytelling
- Top Ten Storied Interview Questions
- The Elevator Pitch Online and Offline
- Ice Breaker Storytelling
- Verbal Graffiti

Interview Storytelling

So far, we've covered the online opportunities for telling your story. Interview storytelling and the elevator pitch (or 60-second commercial) are chances to express your story in person, when your appearance and delivery play a major role. You may tell your story in staff meetings, at dinner parties, social functions, sales meetings, and during live and video interviews. With recruiters in particular, you want to showcase your story and provide a dynamic and engaging 3D picture of your experience and potential. Your personal image and appearance not only have great impact, they tell your story, too.

Stellar image consultant Diana Jennings shares tips on enhancing your visual impact, and includes top interview questions that beg for good stories. Human Resource professionals and recruiters add their comments about storytelling in the interview. Get tips on developing your Elevator Pitch and getting your "Story" down to the bare bones, 60 seconds and cutting out the "verbal graffiti." A feedback form is included so you can be your own critique (video playback) or work with a coach or colleague. This chapter includes a telephone line that lets you record, playback and re-record your elevator pitch until it's perfect.

Interview with an Expert

Diana Jennings is the Founder and President of Brand You Image.

Read her BIO at http://www.visibilitybranding.com or on her site at http://www.brandyouimage.com.

Q: How does your image tell a story about the "Brand Called You?"

A: For some, the "Brand Called You" is a result of their business accomplishments. People like Steve Jobs or Bill Gates are synonymous with the business brands they created. Yet underlying even superstars like Jobs and Gates is the image they project as visionaries. Though casual in their styles, these gentlemen command center stage every time they enter a room. For the rest of us, our image and brand are constant works in progress.

Your image will either support or contradict your story. Developing and refining your image gives you the opportunity to affect others' impression of your level of competence. Have you ever looked at someone when they walk into a room and said that person looks like they're important? Your dress and grooming tells the world "Here I am, take me seriously."

When you enter the room, before you say a word, people are already forming an opinion about you. Think of it this way—if you are looking for a house and drive up a street with homes in good repair with well manicured lawns, you think this is someplace you want to live. Your image similarly shouts out, "This person has his or her act together."

Certain choices will indicate whether or not you pay attention to detail, your eye for quality and your interest in staying current. The thing to remember is not to distract from your objectives by failing to dress and look the part. What if that house had an overgrown front yard and peeling paint? Most people would think twice about stopping for a look inside and if they did look they would most certainly question the asking price.

Think of yourself as a visual storyteller as well as a competent worker. As individuals we have our own styles; it is important that that style and image are consistent with our brand. Another way to think of image and brand is that you are a walking commercial. As with all good ads they satisfy the senses. And with all good ads people are drawn to that brand. In your case that is YOU.

Q: How is your story messaged in your appearance during an interview?

A: Before you've been invited to interview, at least one person has read your BIO, resume or application. You've caught their attention with what's on paper; now they want to know more. They want to see for themselves if you are as good as or better than the image they have in their minds about you as a candidate for the position they're looking to fill.

Does your appearance confirm or contradict what they've read? In less than a minute they will make that decision, and from that point on the interview will be either on track or downhill. Your appearance is a key tool to support your case throughout the interview process. Just because you have the "right clothes" does not mean you are home free. Ill-fitting clothing, poorly-maintained shoes, and sloppy hair or make up will tell the interviewer that attention to detail is likely not one of your strongest attributes. It is common for employers to believe that those who are attentive to personal details are also attentive to the details of their work. In short, if you look the part you increase the odds you will get the position.

How you walk into the room and engage in conversation is another means of a first impression. Something as simple as your grip in a handshake or your level of eye contact indicates your degree of confidence. Your job is to keep the interviewer positively focused on you and what you have to offer, rather than all him or her to be distracted by your appearance or lack of eye contact.

Make certain that your messaging communicates a theme. Do you project consistency throughout your appearance? Are your clothes sending one message (conservative professional), but your hair, grooming and accessories sending another? Let your image reflect the credibility of your brand.

Q: Many first round interviews are conducted online. Do you have any tips or advice for a webcam interview?

A: First and foremost, don't let your guard down. A webcam interview should be treated like a live interview in every respect, with one exception. You are on camera and may be seen by the interviewer even if they are not on camera. You may not think you are being observed but as soon as you are connected you may be observed by someone on the far end.

Treat the camera as if it was the other person in the room. If you are new to using a webcam, record and review a mock interview. This will give you an opportunity to get comfortable with the technology and see what the interviewer will see. A little practice will help in talking to the camera as though it were a person sitting across from you. Look directly into the camera, but don't stare. Relax and be natural as you would in a live interview. The position of your head and body can easily communicate that you mean business or you're uncomfortable with the media. A confident, well-prepared candidate does well live or on camera.

Q: You have worked for major corporate brands both internally and as an image consultant. Would you comment on the importance of aligning your story with that of the corporate brand?

A: Companies look for employees whose brand is aligned with and complementary to the corporate brand. Valued employees, ones that the company cannot afford to lose are those that have been most successful in aligning their own brand with that of their employer. Some people may confuse personal brand alignment with being a "company guy" or a "yes man." In fact, most valued employees challenge the status quo and constantly look for ways to move the company forward. The key thing is that they never lose sight of the company's mission and they use the power of their personal brand to advance the company's agenda. The end result is that they lead by virtue of the brand alignment and get results for both their company and themselves. It is the ultimate career win-win.

Q: Do you have any client stories where there was an image transformation?

A: I once had a financially successful client who "technically" had the right professional wardrobe (suits, jackets, etc.) but her career was stalled. What I uncovered was not only did the details not properly flatter her figure, they also sent conflicting messages. She wasn't being taken seriously about her career path within the organization. Once I taught her how to recognize subtle non-verbal messages and we incorporated the right pieces into her wardrobe, it wasn't long before she had the promotion she was looking for. A polished professional image increases the number of opportunities presented to you, which in turn will increase your chances of becoming successful.

Most people are familiar with the Britain's Got Talent show finalist, Susan Boyle. As soon as she walked onto the stage the camera quickly zoomed in on the eye rolls and snickers coming from the judges and audience members. No one took her seriously and they believed that her talent was going to mimic her unpolished, matronly appearance. Everyone's first impression of her wasn't favorable. Ms. Boyle was fortunate that she had the opportunity to sing and prove everyone's first impression wrong. Not many get that chance. For the rest of us, opportunities can easily disappear if our first impression isn't a positive one.

Diana's top three tips:

1. Familiarize yourself with the company's culture and choose attire that is appropriate and indicates that you take the interview opportunity seriously.

2. Consider the brand attributes communicated in your story and then study your image. Does every detail of your appearance reinforce these qualities?

3. Sending a handwritten thank-you note in appreciation for the interviewer's time speaks highly of your social manners and follow-through.

Top Ten Storied Interview Questions

> "When I have to introduce a high potential candidate over the phone, I like to make a short introduction of less than 30 seconds. If the profile resonates, I then tell more in a 3-minute verbal BIO. I always get an interview for my candidates because my story is clear, simple to understand and matches a current need."
> - Sandrine Joseph, Talent Management Director

These are some of the most often asked questions that are simply "begging" for a story and are a great lead in to the accomplishment stories you have developed using the VBST. Refer back to PART II and the various ways to develop the stories. These questions are behavioral in nature and are meant to elicit "proof of performance" stories. Delivering with clarity and structure, at your comfort level, is not bragging or creating spin but instead factual self promotion. If you need more encouragement and validation on this read *Brag!: The Art of Tooting Your Own Horn without Blowing It* by Peggy Klaus

1. Tell me about a time (story) when you took the lead on a project (Cite leadership areas where you are strong with accompanying story, refer to pie chart in Part II).

2. Tell me about a time (story) when you stuck to a decision or direction you believed in, in spite of opposition.

3. What are your strengths? (Do more than itemize; tell the stories too.)

4. What do you like to do in your free time? (Lead in to your PSR, interests, hobbies, passions.)

5. How would your peers, subordinates, or a previous manager describe you? (Cite references, 360° results, testimonials, LinkedIn recommendations.)

6. Tell me about a situation (story) where you had to work under pressure and meet deadlines.

7. What else should I know about you? (Great lead-in for the accomplishment stories still left untold.)

8. Under what conditions (story) have you taken on more than was required?

9. Tell me about a project (story) you worked on where the requirements changed midstream.

10. Do you have an example (story) of something particularly innovative you have done that made a difference? (Can be in a professional or non-work context.)

Interviewing is "two-way storytelling." The job seeker must tell the interviewer accurate, relevant stories about career achievements and job performance while the interviewer must tell the story of the company, the position and the fit for the job seeker. Don't hesitate in an interview to get the stories around the corporate mission, values, founders and their Corporate Social Responsibility (CSR) initiatives.

The Elevator Pitch Online and Offline

The elevator pitch is your 60-second commercial to message your story. The challenge here is making it clear and concise. The phrase comes from imagining yourself in an elevator with THE person you want to impress: The CEO of the company you want to work for, the recruiter or a coveted client. You step in, the elevator doors shut, you have a captive audience and 100 floors to climb. *What are you going to say?*

Your elevator pitch will play out in a multitude of physical and virtual environments. With 2.O technology there are increasingly innovative ways to network and present your 60-second commercial. One example is BlitzTime, http://www.blitztime.com, which is breaking new ground with a multimedia, interactive networking 60-minute experience like no other. As with many vanguard 2.0 technologies, a free trial is offered. This quick paced, multimedia interaction is an intense and fantastic way to practice and perfect your elevator pitch.

This is how it works: Before the Blitztime event, you can post your profile, photo, even an audio recording, and then view others who will be at the virtual networking. During the first 30 minutes, a topic is covered, often with a guest, then followed by 30 minutes of intense, six-minute virtual one-on-one networking "break-out" sessions on the phone. Participants' screens show the profile (photo, and BIO) of their counterparts. A timer on the screen counts down six minutes, to keep you aware of the time remaining. Whether or not you are finished with your elevator pitch, you are moved to the next six-minute session with another participant. At the end of the hour you have virtually networked with six people. This combination of a webinar followed by networking is a winner and makes for a very impactful live event.

"Using Blitztime to host my series for home-based business owners, I interview guest experts who share knowledge and practical tips to help small business owners thrive. Following the presentation, participants are able to virtually network 1:1. It makes for a great combination."
- Amy Grossman, Founder, Broader Vision,
http://www.broadervision.com

Here is a suggested structure for your 60-second commercial. You can tweak and re-order it, but the basic elements should remain the same and include the following:

Who are you?

What do you do?

Who is your target?

What is their pain, challenge, or need?

What is the hole you are filling?

What is the call to action, follow up, reason to make contact again?

Basic structure to help put your pitch together:

Hello, my name is _____ (include title, company name).

I work with _____ (describe target).

Who experience _____ (challenge, problem).

Which means that _____ the outcome of the problem).

Well, what I do/offer is _____ (describe your product/service).

This means that _____ (the outcome of the solution).

Call to action: Exchange business cards, cite offer, other

Here is one example of the basic information incorporated into a 60-second timeframe. The purpose of the exercise is not to memorize or used verbatim but by writing it down you will gain clarity and structure that will play out in the multitude of scenarios and opportunities where you can re-purpose the content.

My name is _____. I help individuals, who could be executives, entrepreneurs, professionals, MBA participants or consultants, message the story about their personal brand and what makes them unique. My clients can be in career transition or just want to increase their professional visibility online and offline. Their challenge is often how to integrate social media into their communication strategy and writing an effective BIO. I help them in these areas as well as developing a networking strategy with a karma based attitude. Working virtually or onsite in either 1:1 or group sessions, my clients learn how to clearly communicate or tell the story about their personal brand in a compelling way to their target. As a start I offer a complimentary personal brand assessment. Let's exchange contact details.

Here is a feedback form to use on yourself (make a video) or with a coach or colleague. Try and keep it to 60 seconds.

Feedback Form

Timing: Too short _____ Perfect _____ Too long _____

Rate on scale of 1-5 ONE needs work THREE fine FIVE excellent

Greeting (stated name/title/handshake/business card) 1 2 3 4 5

Posture 1 2 3 4 5

Eye Contact 1 2 3 4 5

Structure/Flow/Clarity 1 2 3 4 5

Audible 1 2 3 4 5
Energy/Enthusiasm 1 2 3 4 5
Verbal Graffiti circle Yes No if yes...what? _____
Identify 2 areas to improve _____
Identify 2 good points _____
OVERALL RATING 1 2 3 4 5

Ice Breaker Storytelling

Need to break the ice at a business or social event? Here are three ideas to use to elicit stories from participants; ideas that can play out in a host of situations both professional and informal.

1. USING NAME TAGS

A great way of integrating networking and storytelling is having participants write something about themselves on their name tag that prompts a story and then mingle. Here are some ideas to write on the name tag where, in the mingling process, the stories unfold.

Nickname
Personal motto
An unusual skill or interest
What you would jump out of bed to do at 5:00 AM

2. USING POST-ITS

An alternative is for participants to write one of the above ideas on a post-it, stick it on a wall and invite participants to guess who each one might represent. This also works well after the participants have gotten to know each other for example midway through a workshop or seminar.

3. PROUST PARTY STORYTELLING GAME

Make a good party even better, or play any time with a colleague or friend.

When French novelist and poet Marcel Proust (1871-1922) was still in his teens, there was a fad at parties of asking series of questions that revealed the tastes and aspirations of the guests. Proust's answers showed such insight and maturity that his name has since been associated with the questionnaire. Variations of the Proust questions are also found on sites where you post your profile, and then respond. This, as opposed to standard demographic and work experience information adds "flavor" to your brand. Of note...the last page of each issue of VANITY FAIR features celebrity answers to the Proust questions. In doing so, politicians, actors and authors such as Jane Fonda, Martha Stewart, and Ralph Lauren give us insight into their brands.

Here are the questions:

- What is your current state of mind?
- What do you consider the most overrated virtue?
- On what occasion do you lie?
- What do you most dislike about your appearance?
- Which living person do you most despise?
- What is the quality you most like in a man?
- What is the quality you most like in a woman?
- Which words or phrases do you most overuse?
- What or who is the greatest love of your life?
- When and where were you happiest?
- Which talent would you most like to have?
- If you could change one thing about yourself, what would it be?
- What do you consider your greatest achievement?
- If you were to die and come back as a person or a thing, what would it be?
- Where would you most like to live?

- What is your most treasured possession?
- What do you regard as the lowest depth of misery?
- What is your favorite occupation?
- What is your most marked characteristic?
- What do you most value in your friends?
- Who are your favorite writers?
- Who is your hero of fiction?
- Which historical figure do you most identify with?
- Who are your heroes in real life?
- What are your favorite names?
- What is it that you most dislike?
- What is your greatest regret?

Verbal Graffiti

erbal graffiti is the term used for fillers, non-words, modifiers, condescenders, verbal tics...basically anything that can dilute the message of your storytelling. The first step in eliminating verbal graffiti is to become aware that you are inadvertently diminishing your story. One way is feedback solicited from a coach or colleague. Another way, and often the most effective, is listening to a recording of yourself. Use this Visibility Branding Elevator Pitch Line to do just this where you can record, listen to and re-record a five-minute story segment. This could be your elevator pitch or a response to an interview question. When you press SAVE, it will be sent back to you as a link for reference. Here is the USA number to call: (214) 615-6505 ext. 4737#

Four areas to note during the recording and when listening to others:

1. **FILLER WORDS** (also known as padding or verbal tics)
   - and so on and so forth

- etcetera

- Well,

- To be honest,

- I mean...

- Really?

- Actually

- Frankly

- And (when used as a connector to the next sentence, replacing the period and not giving you and your listeners a much needed break or pause)

2. **NON WORDS:** er, uh, um

3. **QUALIFIERS/MODIFIERS:** These can be a word, a phrase or an entire clause. Semantically, modifiers describe and provide more accurate definitional meaning for another element but often dilute your message and sound timid. Used sparingly, they are okay; just be aware of usage and make sure it's not a consistent practice.

   Examples of how it can dilute your message:

   - I think my strengths lie in the areas of...*vs.* My strengths lie in the areas of....

   - I guess I turned around the situation by...*vs.* I turned around the situation by....

   - I kind of made an impact because...*vs.* I made an impact because....

   - I sort of secured the amount *vs.* I secured the amount.

   - Maybe I should...*vs.* I should....

   - Perhaps I should...*vs.* I should....

4. **CONDESCENDORS** are words used at the end of sentence statements to make sure the audience is following along; but imply they are not. Used too often they sound well...condescending.

- You need to finish this project first, OK?

- After it's signed, return it to us, RIGHT?

- If it's approved we'll move forward, you SEE?

TIPS to eliminate verbal graffiti:

1. Listen to your voicemail messages before sending them.

2. Video yourself; make it private on YouTube.

3. When you feel a run-on sentence coming on PAUSE, take a deep breath and think "PERIOD."

4. Join Toastmasters, a worldwide organization, with a network of 12,500 clubs in 160 countries, in which people learn the arts of speaking, listening and thinking. Search their site for more information and a local chapter http://www.toastmasters.org.

Part V: Writing Your Story Content and the Branded BIO Tool

*DISCOVER * DEVELOP * DISTILL* DIGITIZE * DISSEMINATE * DISCLOSE ** DOCUMENT * DESIGN

Now that you have DEVELOPED and DISTILLED the stories for the content of your BIO, the challenge is to DOCUMENT. Part V focuses on developing copy that can be adapted in various versions of your written story, for corporate or personal, online and offline use. The difference between a resume and a BIO is defined. Interviews with experts cover effective BIO usage and placement for authors, professional speakers and for business plans. Writing guidelines from a copywriter help to craft your BIO. Then, a personal branding coach describes how to internationalize your BIO, using examples from a successful global professional, executive and diplomat. A designer and personal brand strategist offers comprehensive visual presentation guidelines for a one-page BRANDED BIO with visual impact, branding and consistency, and then performs a "makeover" taking a BIO from "adequate" to a compelling BRANDED BIO. Last, you'll use the BIO DEPOT as your storytelling adventures evolve, to re-purpose existing content, track the evolution and to create more versions to captivate your target.

- The BIO
- BIO Usage and Placement
- Resume versus the BIO
- Resume to BIO morphs
- Writing Guidelines and Top Ten Tips
- Internationalizing Your BIO
- Visual Guidelines and the Branded BIO
- BIO GEMS
- The BIO Depot
- Action Verbs
- Conclusion

The BIO

The BIO is the written version of your story.

"The best LinkedIn Summaries are engaging and tell stories that help others understand your professional capabilities. No part of the LinkedIn Profile gives you as much freedom. When asked, "What's the biggest mistake you see on LinkedIn?," the first thing that comes to mind is a weak or incomplete Summary."
- Jason Alba, Author, *I'm on LinkedIn—Now What???*
http://www.JibberJobber.com

he word BIO is a derivative of the word BIOGRAPHY which means story. So what do branding strategists and recruiters mean by the BIO? Is it a biographical sketch? A profile? A narrative? A summary statement? Answer...your BIO is the written version of your story. Like a chameleon that changes color to adapt to its environment, the storied content you develop is adapted, tweaked and re-purposed to the target, placement and usage.

This section talks about various versions of your BIO that you can craft. It introduces the BIO TOOL, a highly recommended document to have in your brand Toolkit, which can be used as a stand-alone document (most cases), or as a complement to your resume. This is not something you want to throw together at the last minute. It showcases your writing skills and should be prepared carefully. Crafting your brand message will take time, reflection, proofing and editing. You may want to work with a professional in crafting yours.

Your BIO is one of many brand "touch points" you have with your stakeholders. Having storied content to post online or for offline purposes is essential whether you are a professional, executive, entrepreneur, solo-preneur, coach, artist, musician, or recent graduate.

You have revealed the stories and "mini-stories" related to your key ac-complishments, emotional intelligence and leadership skills, interests, values, volunteer activities, your PSR (Personal Social Responsibility) and more. You can now message these in your written storied content and truly come "alive."

"I use mini BIOs in my communications with other HR colleagues inside my company: storytelling is a good way to remain focused on the strengths of an executive and make his/her career go faster by reaching the relevant people from inside and sometimes outside. It's a central tool in professional networking."
- Sandrine Joseph, HR Talent Management Director

BIO Usage and Placement

Ten Ways to Use Your BIO

NOTE: Before using your BIO for any of the below purposes ALWAYS look at it with a critical eye and consider the TARGET. Adapt and tweak if necessary.

---

1. To post on online networking sites such as LinkedIn (place in SUMMARY statement), Viadeo, FaceBook, Xing and on alumni, club and professional association sites.

2. For presentation or speech purposes to give to the person who will be introducing you. This will not only be appreciated but is often expected.

3. After a networking event, send as an attachment with your follow up message.

4. Send in advance of an initial meeting. This can save a lot of time, as once you do meet you can "cut to the chase."

5. Post on your personal website and/or blog.

6. To include in your business plan.

7. As an author, you will need numerous versions of your BIO.

8. To use instead of a resume in particular for musicians, writers, consultants and other professions.

9. Consider sending with your resume to round it out and "soften" the edges.

10. Starting a new job, circulate to your team as an introduction.

> "I search for candidates on LinkedIn and read the summary statements. Most I find are too short to give me any insight and are just a few bullet points summarizing the resume. It takes a lot of effort to write, but a strong profile, especially building out the summary, is worth it. A good profile will make you distinctive and increase your chances of being contacted by recruiters. In a world where it's getting harder to differentiate between professionals and where companies are becoming more demanding, cutting and pasting a few points from your resume will not make you stand out from the crowd."
> - Annalisa Riches, Senior European HR Business Partner at Sabre and lastminute.com

Interview with Experts on BIO Usage

Speaking Engagements

Janice Nagourney is Director at Thought Leaders International, France, and sources high-level professional speakers for major corporate events across Europe, Asia and the USA.

Read her BIO at http://www.visibilitybranding.com or on her site http://www.thoughtleadersinternational.com.

Q: How do you see the importance of the BIO for speaking purposes?

A: A good BIO is an excellent sales tool. It highlights your strengths and relevant background, including books you've written and talks you've given. It is different in form and purpose from the CV you would use in a job search.

Q: How is the BIO used by professional speakers?

A: Professional speakers spend time on crafting a BIO which is concise and easy to read. Unless the topics in your speaking portfolio are radically different, a single well-written BIO is sufficient.

Q: Is the BIO used to introduce the speaker at an event?

A: Normally, for introductory purposes, professional speakers provide the client with a concise introduction which in a way is a much shortened version of their longer BIO. Ideally just a few phrases in length, this introduction piece can be read by the person introducing you with a text that "sets the stage" appropriately. It can also be handed out and included in conference material.

Q: What else is part of a professional speaker's "Story Kit?"

A: An easy to navigate website, which provides hi-resolution photos for use in printed material, links to one or more videos, a speaker BIO, a speaker CV and a suggested introduction for clients to use when presenting you.

BIO in the Business Plan

Amy Grossman is a One Page Business Plan certified consultant, Coach and Author and helps solo-entrepreneurs and founders of non-profit organizations with their business plans.

Read her BIO at http://www.visibilitybranding.com or on her site: http://www.broadervision.com.

Q: How does the BIO feature in a Business Plan?

A: The BIO brings to life the company's vision and mission by adding a personal dimension. The size and scope of your business plan determines the role the BIO plays. Long, formal business plans call for a formal BIO. Single-page business plans call for a simpler BIO.

Q: What are the key elements to message?

A: To accompany a single page business plan, your BIO can include your unique selling proposition, brand statement or tag line along with your picture. It should also include relevant training, and what earlier experience drew you to the work you do.

Q: Why is the BIO important?

A: People do business with people they know, like and trust. The BIO is an introduction and is the first step in building trust. It also qualifies you for the work by establishing your credentials in a storytelling format. For companies with a management team, the BIO of each senior executive is positioned to highlight specific functional specialties. Together, the BIOs present the broad skill set that will move the business forward. Outside investors consider the management team one of the most important factors in deciding to invest in a company.

Q: Where should the BIO be placed?

A: For a short business plan, a BIO is an essential add-on. Have your BIO, picture and contact information on a page that is attached to your business plan. For business plans that are longer than 20 pages, the BIO appears in the "Management Team" section of the plan.

Q: What resources can you recommend?

A: For a free One Page Business Plan Starter Kit, go to http://www.broadervision.com. For an outline for a 20+ page business plan, go to http://www.ntia.doc.gov/opadhome/mtdpweb/busplano.htm.

BIO in the MBA Application

Alexander Kumming, Founder of Strong Education and MBACube, helps individuals from around the world with the application process to enter leading full-time and Executive MBA programs in the USA and Europe.

Read his BIO at http://www.visibilitybranding.com or on his site: http://www.mbacube.com.

Q: What are the typical questions on an application that speak to a person's "story?"

A: Although the specific questions on school applications vary, schools generally seek to discover the following "stories" about a candidate:

Identity: Who are you professionally and personally? What are your values and drivers? What are your meaningful experiences (accomplishments and failures).

Future Goals: What are your short and long-term goals? How and why have these goals been formulated?

Motivation & Fit: Why have you made the decision to pursue the MBA at this point in your life and career? Why are you interested in our school and how will you fit in and contribute to the school community?

Q: How effective is "storytelling" in the MBA application process?

A: Storytelling is vital in the sense that great applications weave together a variety of anecdotes and life experiences in a way that consistently and credibly supports the themes and message that the candidate wants to convey. Good essays entertain and educate the reader while credibly transmitting the message and qualities of the candidate.

Q: Any tips on writing a good story?

A: Looking at typical MBA profiles and the sheer number of capable people applying, candidates can get discouraged: "There's nothing special about me. I'm just an ordinary manager (or consultant, engineer, analyst, entrepreneur)." In effect, there are many other people applying. But there is only one you. Good planning and storytelling discern your particular talent, professional development, and vision that will uniquely contribute to the MBA course.

While choosing the content of the stories is important, the reasons why this content is chosen are even more so. What are the meaning, insights, and life or professional lessons that the stories convey? What is the vision of future and self that these stories give? In other words, the WHY is often more relevant than the WHAT.

BIO Usage for Authors

Mitchell Levy is the author of eleven business books and the CEO and Executive Editor of the independent publishing house Happy About.

Read his BIO at http://www.visibilitybranding.com or on his site: http://www.happyabout.info.

Q: You have worked with close to 100 authors and are an author yourself. You've seen over 2,500 BIOs. What is the importance of the BIO in publishing a book?

A: It's the first thing I look at, and terribly important. Three things we evaluate when making a publishing decision:

1. Credibility of the author.
2. Whether the book will be good.
3. Whether the author can market it.

The BIO is the key element viewed to answer the first question, and helps address the other responses. We'll often search on URLs within the author's BIO (or Google the appropriate names) to verify the quality of the work and capability of the author. From the reader's perspective, it's the second thing they look at, the first being the topic.

Q: How many versions of the BIO are needed and where is the place-ment?

A: For us, we need 3-5 versions of the BIO based on where it will be used:

1. Web
2. Inside the book
3. Blog
4. Radio
5. Print

Based on the audience, the BIO needs to be tailored slightly to address the needs of the audience reading it.

Q: What makes an effective BIO for an author?

A: The BIO needs to quickly and efficiently establish the author as an expert on the topic of the book. There are many ways to show expertise, but the reader of the BIO must say, "Yes, I can learn from this author!"

Q: How important is the BIO in the marketing of a book and how does it feature?

A: The BIO is a tool the author uses to help bond with an audience. If a prospective buyer is looking at a title, it is important to position the author as someone they'd want to read. When deciding between three or four books on the same topic, the two key elements the reader will look at include the footprint of the book and the BIO.

Resume Versus the BIO

he RESUME and the BIO can be complementary or stand alone tools. In any case, they are "must haves" in your brand toolkit. If you already have a great resume with a powerful summary or profile statement as a header, then start with this foundation as backbone content and integrate into your BIO.

A strong Summary or Profile Statement at the top of your resume is KEY. Why? You have heard of the Pareto Principle or the 80–20 rule which states that for many phenomena, 80% of the consequences stem from 20% of the causes. This is the case for the summary/profile statement. Up to 80% of the impact of your resume is in the summary statement. A survey of hiring managers, recruiters and human resource managers indicates that if the summary statement is weak or non-existent there is less likelihood that the whole resume will be read. Ninety-percent polled said they do not read the entire resume. For this reason the summary/profile statement has to be well crafted. It is key because it is an information-rich snapshot, providing a foundation and overview of what you have accomplished.

The resume is a recognized and requested document, chronological by definition. It might be a stretch to say the traditional resume is "dead" but statistics reveal that it is no longer the primary source of information used by recruiters and HR professionals. There are, however, innovative ways of making it more "storied" in your summary/profile statement. There is not one standard way to craft this statement, so be creative!

Excellent examples where the use of quotes, EQ, leadership skills, and volunteer activities are messaged can be found in the book *Happy About My Resume* by Barbara Safani, the EXPERT interviewed next.

Interview with an Expert

Barbara Safani is Founder of Career Solvers and has 15 years of experience in career management, recruiting, and executive coaching. Her book *Happy About My Resume* gives more than 30 examples.

Read her BIO at http://www.visibilitybranding.com or on her site: http://www.careersolvers.com.

Q: What is the difference between a RESUME and a BIO?

A: A RESUME is used when applying to an open position. It supplies education, work experience and achievements chronologically. The BIO is a more flexible document that is written in narrative format. It focuses on career progression and accomplishment highlights, so as to tell a story about the candidate. It is often used to add value to a candidate profile or present his/her background in a different way.

Q: When do you use a BIO?

A: You can use a BIO as part of a candidate portfolio, packaged with other marketing collateral such as a resume and cover letter. BIOs are used on many online identity and business/social networking sites. A BIO should also be included in a business plan, on a company or personal website, or on a blog.

Q: Does the BIO replace the resume?

A: No. Employers still expect to see a RESUME when recruiting for open positions; however the BIO quickly communicates the candidate's value proposition in a narrative format, and can be used to help a hiring manager make a more informed decision about a candidate.

Q: Who needs a BIO?

A: Today, everyone needs a branded BIO, for the reasons mentioned.

Q: Are the BIO and the RESUME complementary?

A: Yes. People absorb information in different ways. Some prefer to read a structured document such as a resume with chronological order. Others prefer to hear the story behind the candidate's evolution in a particular field or industry, and the narrative format of the BIO is perfect for this.

Resume to BIO Morphs

EXAMPLE #1 Resume PROFILE/SUMMARY Statement morphed into a BIO. (Name is fictitious.)

RESUME PROFILE STATEMENT

International Senior Marketing Management Professional with over 15 years experience in strategic development, brand management, driving global product launches and integrated marketing communication campaigns. Positions held in the US and Taiwan with Proctor & Gamble, Pfizer and PepsiCo with progressive responsibility and leadership, managing multicultural teams across regions. Strong track record consistently exceeding business goals and objectives. Twice selected for high potential corporate programs. Bilingual (English and Chinese) with an MBA in International Management.

BIO

Frank Chen is a bilingual International Senior Marketing Management Professional with over 15 years experience in strategic development, brand management, driving global product launches and integrated marketing communication campaigns. Currently, he is Director at Proctor & Gamble and is based at the US headquarters. Frank has held positions in the consumer health care and well-being sectors with P&G, Pfizer and PepsiCo, with progressive responsibility and leadership, managing multicultural teams across regions. With all three of these leading corporations, he has been recognized with awards for his strong track record, consistently exceeding business goals and objectives. Additionally, he was twice selected for high potential corporate international management programs.

Frank grew up in Taiwan and spent over three years in the US in college (MBA) and at work. A passion for baseball, as more than a spectator, was ignited during his youth. He has received awards as a star pitcher at the National Baseball Championship level. Frank envisions his future career taking on more scope and scale at the international level, drawing upon his leadership skills and strategic business acumen. He feels that challenges are wonderful opportunities to navigate, using strategic vision, knowledge, experience and influence to lead the way to attain individual and organizational goals.

EXAMPLE #2 Resume PROFILE/SUMMARY Statement morphed into a BIO

RESUME PROFILE STATEMENT

Multilingual manager with over 10 years experience as a specialist in business development, public relations and event management. Team player with strong interpersonal skills, accustomed to taking initiative and working with stakeholders at the highest level. Expertise in written and oral communications. Academic credentials include a Master's Degree in Computer Science and Business with certifications in project management (PMP) and finance.

BIO

Laila Kamoun is a multilingual international program manager with over 10 years experience in the network communication industry. With a unique combination of proven analytical and leadership skills, she has held senior-level roles, managing virtual cross-cultural and functional teams across eight countries. Academic credentials include a Master's Degree in Computer Science and Business with certifications in project management (PMP) and finance. Laila is considered an intrapreneur-entrepreneur within an organization, with an ability to deliver on a wide spectrum of subjects such as process change, supply chain as well as technology. She has a proven track record in building solutions from business case to deployment and creating win-win relationships with partners. Multilingual, Laila speaks fluent English, French, Italian and Arabic.

Key Attributes: self motivated, results oriented, problem solver and people focused.

Value Add: turning problems into opportunities and international cultural understanding.

Writing Guidelines and Ten Top Tips

> **"As an HR Talent Management Director I ask all executives who want to see me for career advice or a promotion to write a mini-BIO of themselves (200 words max) and a CV (2 pages max). A good storyteller is often a great leader. He/she knows where his/her strengths are, how to communicate on them and how to then engage people to follow him/her."**
> **- Sandrine Joseph, Talent Management Director**

eveloping BIO content and then crafting your written BIO can be challenging. As you have learned, there are many online and offline situations in which your written story is required or requested. Preparing various versions is indispensable. In some cases, you may wish to hire a professional to help you as it needs to be well written with a good structure and flow. For the Do It Yourself-ers (DIYers), we introduce Lynda Sydney, the Wonder Wordsmith herself and expert copywriter with her advice and tips:

Top Ten Tips for Writing Your BIO by Lynda Sydney

1. **Order information based on what will resonate with your target.**

   This is KEY! The beauty of the BIO is that it does not have to be chronological as compared to the resume, which is chronological by definition.

2. **Use the third person.**

   This means to write as if someone else is talking about you—imagine being introduced in a meeting or at a speaking engagement. Use your name and the pronouns he/she or his/hers instead of I/me.

3. **Include your first and last name in the first sentence.**

   If you use a nickname, give your full name with the nickname in parentheses. You can then use the nickname throughout the rest of your BIO.

   Example:
   Charles (Chuck) Stone
   Christina T. (Chris) Anderson

4. **The first paragraph should have impact.**

   Attract the reader's attention by listing high profile companies and credentials with a high level cumulative background summary.

   Executive Example: Chris Grant's 15-year international career in the investment and venture capital arena is best described as following a building block trajectory. After a degree from HEC, a top management school in Europe, he launched his career with Société Générale followed by JPMorgan and then Montgomery Securities. This 10-year experience in corporate environments took place on both sides of the Atlantic in major financial centers: New York, London, Paris and Luxembourg.

   Entrepreneur Example: Cecile Hasroyan, Image Consultant and Founder of CecileH, has over 22 years experience in the world of fashion, style and image consulting. Starting as a model with an international agency, she drew inspiration from stylists, makeup artists, designers and hairdressers from around the world. She applied her academic studies in Communication as she transitioned into press relations and event management, spending more than 10 years in strategic communication roles. Cecile has organized press and international events for a large fashion group.

For the rest of her story see http://www.cecileh.com.

Academic Example: Angel Cabrera is President of Thunderbird School of Global Management, widely recognized as the Number 1 school of International Business. For over 60 years, Thunderbird has been dedicated to developing leaders with the global mindset, business skills, entrepreneurial spirit and social responsibility necessary to create real, sustainable value for their organizations, communities and the world. Dr. Cabrera is a world-renowned global leader and management educator whose work and expertise has been recognized and tapped by top international organizations.

For the rest of Dr. Cabrera's story, see http://www.thunderbird.edu/about_thunderbird/faculty/faculty _alphabetical/_206656.htm.

5. **Include languages and academic credentials.**

If you speak multiple languages or have earned a college degree, be sure to include these in your BIO.

Example: Susan holds an MBA from Thunderbird School of Global Management and certification as a Reach Personal Brand Strategist, Online Identity Expert and 360°Reach Assessment Analyst. She is fluent in French and English, and has a working knowledge of German.

6. **Mention brand names that will resonate.**

If you have worked for a well-known company with a household name you will want to include them here—Microsoft, Sears, Google, etc. If you've worked at smaller companies, you can simply reference your expertise in the specific industry.

Example: Lindsey Tramuta is a bilingual communications and marketing professional with experience in branding and luxury mar-keting. At Landor Associates, the leading global branding agency, she worked with clients such as Citroën, Kraft, P&G, and L'Oréal and was able to apply practical applications of her theoretical course-work. She completed her academic degrees in the United States and France, most recently receiving a Master's Degree in Global Communications. Lindsey's unique and diverse educational and professional background has equipped her with the necessary analytical, research and writing skills for the field of Communications. This is coupled with her enthusiasm to continue learning and expand her professional experience. Lindsey is now exploring opportunities to build her professional career.

For the rest of Lindsey's story see her LinkedIn profile: http://fr.linkedin.com/in/lindsey588.

7. **Mention important achievements.**

Include your awards, publications and professional organizations to which you belong, with a link to the website if possible.

8. **Add a photo.**

See the next section where this is covered in detail.

9. **LENGTH of your BIO**

Following are the three recommended lengths of your BIO to have ready to resonate with your target. Be aware that no version of your BIO is a static document. Each time you place your BIO, look at it with a FRESH eye from your TARGET'S perspective, and tweak, polish or repurpose accordingly.

MINI - 140 characters. You in a nutshell. This is also the maximum length for a TWITTER profile. Make it succinct and snappy, using words that telegraph WHO, WHAT, and WHY.

SHORT - 100–150 words. The length often requested for speaking engagements and association profiles.

LONG - 2000 characters, the maximum allowed for a LinkedIn Summary Statement. This long, more narrative BIO version will be roughly three to five paragraphs and will not exceed one page. Start with a high level cumulative paragraph followed by themed paragraphs that focus on a particular area.

10. Include your contact information.

Email and telephone are the basics but also consider your SKYPE address, Twitter, LinkedIn, website and blog links and, if it makes sense, your Second Life avatar name.

Sample lead-in sentence starters for the BIO

1. A 15-year career in _____ has taken [name] to Asia, Europe and the US where she/he held senior level positions in _____ and _____.

2. For the last X years, [name] has helped companies to accelerate growth in new markets around the globe.

3. [Name] is a frequent speaker at prestigious international forums, and his/her views about global leadership, business education and corporate citizenship are often quoted by leading world media, including _____.

4. [Name] has a unique combination of skills that enable her/him to _____.

5. [Name] is a multi-lingual _____ professional with over X years of experience in _____.

6. Key projects during her/his career evolved around _____.

7. [Name] manages all aspects of _____ including _____, _____ and _____.

8. A sought after speaker, her/his media engagements include _____ and he/she has been featured in _____.

9. Earlier in her/his career [name] worked as a _____ where she/he _____.

10. [Name] is an entrepreneurial executive who has consistently _____.

11. [Name] enjoys when he/she can combine his/her passion for _____ with _____.

12. Prior to founding _____, she/he _____.

13. An experienced trainer and facilitator, [name] designs international team building workshops in corporate and academic environments.

14. Recognized for his/her experience and knowledge in the field of entrepreneurship, [name] was asked to _____.

15. With more than X years of _____ experience, [name] brings a wealth of knowledge to her/his role as _____.

Finally, get FEEDBACK from colleagues and friends.

Give your BIO to a few people to read. Besides proofreading, ask them about the presentation of the material—is it clear, is the writing compelling, does it make them want to continue reading? Is it an accurate reflection of who you are and what you have done? Are there any specific details or information you've missed? Encourage them to be candid and take any suggestions constructively.

As an extension to this chapter, contact Lynda at <u>lsydney@sympatico.ca</u> for a complementary guide that gives more tips, advice and examples of grammar, punctuation usage and common errors that are specific to writing excellent content for your BIO. Includes tips on usage of the following:

- Apostrophes
- Dashes
- Ellipses
- Hyphens
- Numbers
- Quotation Marks
- Overused Words and Alternatives
- Credentials
- American/British Differences

BIO

Lynda is a freelance advertising copywriter from Toronto, Canada. She has a solid agency background, having worked in both account management and creative, and began freelancing full-time in 2001. Her passion for Paris inspired her to spend several months in the City of Light to network and investigate her options in making a move to Paris. Since 2005 she has been working with clients in both Paris and Toronto.

Site: http://www.lyndasydney.com
Blog: http://www.CarChick.ca

Internationalizing Your BIO

How to Write an Internationally Focused BIO
By Megan Fitzgerald, Expat Career and Personal Branding Coach

As an expat career and personal branding coach, Megan Fitzgerald draws from 15+ years of experience supporting professionals and entrepreneurs worldwide. In this chapter she will be providing actionable guidance and examples on how to write an international BIO that will position you as the candidate of choice for any globally-focused career, or the provider of choice serving a global market.

Topics covered in this section include:

- Why internationalize your BIO?

- Key experience, qualities, and skills sought

- Keywords

- The importance of addressing culture

- BIO Examples (C-Level Executive, Professional, Diplomat, Entrepreneur)

- Additional Resources

Why Internationalize Your BIO?

It may go without saying that having an internationally focused BIO is a must if you want to be seriously considered for jobs overseas.

But in an increasingly competitive and global marketplace, even if you are not looking to work abroad, having a more international profile can help you stand out and strengthen your application for many types of positions. As more businesses are engaging outside of their own country's borders and managing virtual, global teams becomes more common, some employers now consider the ability to work across cultures as a required—not just desired—skill set.

There is evidence supporting the fact that "global citizens" are seen as more desirable—and hence more hireable—due to certain skill sets acquired as a result of their international experience. One study conducted by INSEAD (a top business school in France) and the Kellogg School of Management (a top business school in the US) reported that people who live abroad have been shown to be not only more creative, but are better negotiators and can more readily "think out of the box." So not only will internationalizing your BIO help you stand out but it will also help increase the perceived value you would bring to any organization.

If you are an entrepreneur serving the global market place, your prospective clients living in other countries will want to be sure that you are able to work across cultures, particularly with their culture. Demonstrating your international experience will help build trust and confidence in your ability to serve the global community.

As you can see, there are real benefits to adding an international dimension to the "story" that is your BIO.

Desired Experience, Qualities and Skills

Employers hiring for internationally-focused positions, or consumers looking for service providers with global experience, generally seek many of the following skills and qualities:

- Cultural sensitivity

- Flexibility and adaptability

- Positive attitude and resilience

- Cross-cultural communication skills

- Language skills

- Writing skills

- Comfort level in multicultural or unfamiliar environments

- Specific technical knowledge or expertise that is not present in the target market

- International travel and experience (paid, volunteer, short and long term, internships)

- Multicultural experience in your home country

- Study abroad or exchange program experiences

- Attending international conferences

- Contributing to international publications or media

I encourage you to sit down and write out stories about any of these qualities or experiences so that you can bring them to life when writing your BIO.

Keywords

Recent studies show that employers (more than 45%) and recruiters (more than 80%) use the Internet to find potential hires. Hence you are more likely to be found online by those sourcing candidates for internationally-focused positions if your BIO online includes keywords that match the keywords used in their search engine queries.

In the same vein, if you are running a business that serves the global market, it's important to have the right keywords in your BIO to attract traffic to your website and build confidence in your prospective clients that you work well with people of different cultures.

Here are some examples of keywords you can use to "internationalize" your BIO and help you get found online:
culture, cultural, cross cultural, international, global, names of foreign cities, countries and continents, world, worldwide, bilingual, trilingual, multilingual, names of international organizations or companies, names of international professional associations, names of international publications and media, developing world, developing economies, travel, fluent, fluency

The Importance of Culture

As 'cultural fit' is an important part of evaluating a candidate being considered for an internationally-focused position or a potential service provider, it's important that your BIO be written in a culturally appropriate fashion. This means ensuring the skills and qualities valued most by the culture(s) in which you will be working or serving, as well as some of their cultural values, are clearly communicated.

Here are some examples of taking culture into account when writing your BIO:

- Japanese employers are not looking for people who can come in and create change or generate quick results. They are looking for team players they can train or who they can work with well to achieve their goals. Team achievement is more celebrated than individual achievement. So be sure that a team-orientation comes through loud and clear in your BIO if you are looking for a job in Japan. If you are a business serving the Japanese market, your focus should also be less on individual and more on team or community achievements or success.

- Australian employers and consumers are likely to be more concerned with your demonstrating your experience and ability to do a job with a positive, can-do attitude than the right degree so your BIO should reflect that. But if you look at South African employers and consumers, you'll find they consider post secondary school education and credentials very important when evaluating candidates and service providers. So be sure to list all relevant education and credentials in your BIO.

- Italian employers and consumers are looking to hire enthusiastic, dynamic people, so that energy should come out in your BIO. But if you are looking for a job in Germany or serving the German market, it would be more appropriate to keep your writing very concise, clear and to the point due to their focus on accuracy and efficiency.

- Decision-making by consensus is common in Sweden, so describing yourself as highly motivated or ambitious will not position you as a good cultural fit with a Swedish employer or consumer. While in the UK, it is important to emphasize your achievements so action-oriented words would be valued. Humor is also a very important part of British culture, so throwing in a bit of British-like wit could also help to position you as a good fit culturally.

BIO Examples

I'm sharing some of my clients' BIOs to provide examples illustrating the points I have made in this section. Steps were taken to use certain keywords and highlight specific key skills, qualities and experience. The target culture(s) also played a role in determining which aspects of their skills and experience were emphasized to ensure the BIO was culturally appropriate. In some cases the client chose to share personal information to support their case for being a strong candidate.

Executive

Fernando Samaniego
Spanish Executive currently based in Dubai, United Arab Emirates
Transition from Traditional to Digital Media Expert

Fernando Samaniego is an international new media strategist with 15+ years of experience on four continents in building and transforming media companies into thriving centers of profitable innovation. With his experienced, global perspective and keen understanding of social and technical trends, he keeps companies on the cutting edge and front lines of changing how we live, work and communicate.

Fernando is known for building high performance global teams and collaborative organizational cultures to transform companies from market players to recognized market leaders. It's the powerful combination of his future-oriented vision and rigorous analysis that has helped companies struggling to adapt to challenging social and technological changes redefine how they do business. He has leveraged Greenfield, M&A and organic growth strategies and quick to market execution to create sustainable growth. He has turned around failing companies in the face of decreasing income, large debt and economic recessions.

As a multilingual, multicultural, forward-thinking intrapreneur, he has an incredible breadth and depth of industry experience. He's worked with organizations across the globe in all areas of media including newspapers, magazines, television, radio, mobile, Internet, news, classifieds and portals. His pioneering work in developing new business models and strategies has garnered media attention and has influenced industry best practices.

An MBA and thought leader in his field, Fernando's work and articles have been featured in industry publications including Les Clés de la Presse (Poland), iWorld (Spain), Les Clés de la Presse (France) and ABC (Spain). He also regularly presents at media conferences and events, including the Publishing Expo in Russia, Media Institute Conference in France, and the Mundo Internet 2.0 Congress in Spain.

In this first BIO an evaluation is made based on the factors identified as important when internationalizing your BIO:

Keywords: international, worldwide, global, multilingual, multicultural, names of specific countries (UAE, Spain, France, Russia, Poland), names of global publications (IWorld, Les Clés de la Presse), names of international events (such as Mundo Internet 2.0 Congress)

Skills and Attributes: cross-cultural communication, cultural sensitivity, flexibility, adaptability, entrepreneurial, works well in multicultural environments, builds global teams, strong writing and presentation skills

Experience: Over 15 years experience with companies worldwide (on four continents) in all areas of the media, helping them leverage new media and cutting-edge strategies to transform them into market leaders, MBA

Languages: Multilingual.

Publications: He's been published in publications in France, Spain, and Poland.

Events: He's presented at industry events in Russia, France, and Spain.

Culture: At the time of the writing of this BIO, Fernando was located in the United Arab Emirates. So it was with this culture in mind that the BIO was written. The United Arab Emirates has a diverse, multicultural and highly cosmopolitan society, with over 80% of its inhabitants being expatriates. Despite work permit challenges, employers in the UAE tend to embrace that multiculturalism. They generally like more detail about your professional background and accomplishments and value people with more education or degrees. The mention of his MBA, key professional accomplishments and his multicultural experience support that cultural profile.

Professional

Roberta Zelari
Italian professional currently based in Al Ain, United Arab Emirates
International Human Resources Specialist

Roberta is an international human resources expert specializing in international recruitment, cross cultural intermediation, project management and manpower planning. She uses her natural ability to connect across cultures and a dynamic, collaborative approach to manage challenges, optimize change and empower companies to use their human resources to drive innovation and accelerate business growth.

With 10+ years experience in human resources in various environments, from multinational companies to start-ups, from local to global projects, she has led stand-alone missions and achieved business objectives by managing both local and international teams. Having lived and/or worked in more than 20 countries and speaking three languages, she enjoys working in culturally diverse, international companies and communities. She thrives in face-paced, dynamic environments and is passionate about technology and developing new systems and solutions. Given her strong problem solving and facilitation skills, she is often selected to pioneer projects in challenging or new environments and manage virtual teams.

A committed lifelong learner with a degree in International Relations and extensive training in management, facilitation and negotiation, Roberta is a certified Targeted Selection Interviewer and Predictive Index Survey Analyst. She is also a member of several human resource professional associations, including the Society for Human Resources Management, the Human Capital Institute, and Associazione Italiana per la Direzione del Personale.

As a global and socially responsible citizen, Roberta supports Medecins Sans Frontiers and Computer Aid International. When off duty, she loves traveling, scuba diving, discovering new places and cultures, watching films, reading, and receiving friends at home to show them her collection of world maps.

Diplomat

Mehdi Drissi
Moroccan diplomat currently based in Paris, France
Head of the United Nation's Food and Agriculture Organization's (UN FAO)
Information Office for France, Benelux and Monaco

Mehdi Drissi is a global alliance and management specialist passionate about connecting with key decision makers to generate extraordinary results. Based in Paris, France, he is currently head of the United Nation's FAO Information Office for France, Benelux and Monaco. It's his natural ability to communicate across cultures, masterfully negotiate agreements, and strategically manage events and projects that equips him to build powerful alliances, generate excitement and inspire people to action.

Over his 20-year career in international education, culture and diplomacy, he has developed programs and events which have increased awareness of French culture and sport, increased registration in French universities and cultural programs, and strengthened political and business partnerships across the globe. Mehdi has negotiated bilateral and multilateral agreements between countries and parties often reticent to collaborate, succeeding where others have failed.

With three degrees, the ability to speak six languages and having lived and/or worked in over 53 countries, Mehdi has also built an extensive network of journalists and media contacts. It is his understanding of different media environments, which allow him to communicate with maximum impact. He has an exceptional track record of superior global program and event management, and of working with high profile leaders in education, politics, sports, and business worldwide.

Entrepreneur

Jason Pitelli
CEO of Love4Adventure,
Travel company which provides thought-provoking tours worldwide

Jason Pittelli is the CEO (Chief Explorations Officer) of Love4Adventure. It is his passion for adventure that inspires the engaging, thought-provoking travel experiences he and his team of guides provide to his guests. They bring the history of the Eternal City of Rome and numerous cities around the globe alive in daily tours for travelers.

In his entertaining and highly interactive style, Jason weaves together stories about people and myths from the past and relates them to modern-day life. His guests leave with a better understanding of the people and events that shape a city and a tangible connection to the past. For the traveler with a thirst for more than just a history lesson, Love4Adventure's tours are an indispensable component to any holiday.

Jason and his guides engage their guests in a way that draws on their own experiences to better understand the world around them. They have an enthusiastic, personable and easy-to-follow approach making a potentially daunting experience at the Vatican Museum or Sistine Chapel accessible, interesting, and fun.

With over eight years of experience as a professional tour guide, Jason has visited 40 countries on six continents and traveled over 60,000 miles (100,000 kms). He has been river rafting and caving in Laos, explored the Amazonian rainforest of Bolivia, and braved the freezing waters off South Africa to swim amongst great white sharks. His passion for adventure knows no bounds.

It is this endless desire for new and exciting experiences, as well as his natural ability to teach, inspire and entertain, that make Love4Adventure more than just a tour company. Love4Adventure is built on Jason's vision of helping others learn more about themselves and the world through travel.

Additional Cultural Resources:

- *When Cultures Collide: Living Across Cultures* by Richard Lewis
- CultureActive http://www.cultureactive.com, a website with a multimedia Cultural Profiler based on the Lewis Model of Culture.
- Culture Crossing http://www.culturecrossing.net, a website on cross-cultural etiquette and communication styles, allowing you to connect with expatriates worldwide.
- Expat-Blog http://www.expat-blog.com a website which gives access to over 5,000 blogs written by expatriates so you can learn firsthand how to engage across cultures.

BIO

Megan Fitzgerald is an expat career and personal branding coach and the founder of *Career by Choice*. With 15+ years experience in professional and business development in over 20 countries on five continents, she has helped expatriates worldwide use their personal brand to build a career or business to support their life abroad. She leverages her extensive training and global experience and a creative 2.0 approach to help these global minds uncover and communicate their unique value online and offline and realize success on their own terms. Named one of the top 50 personal branding consultants worth working with, she has been featured in Fortune Small Business Magazine, CNN Money.com, Wall Street Journal Online, and several other books and publications. She is a contributing author to several books including *Storytelling about Your Brand Online & Offline* and the *Twitter Job Search Guide*.

For the rest of Megan's story, see: http://www.careerbychoice.com.

Visual Guidelines and the Branded BIO

By Sue Brettell, http://www.suebrettell.com, Personal Branding Designer and Copywriter

Congratulations! You've finished writing your BIO...now what?

So far this book has concentrated on the content of your BIO and getting it written. Now, go beyond simply adding a photo to your plain BIO and create a BRANDED BIO that exudes your individuality. By developing your own visual identity and applying a few design and layout principles, you will ensure your BIO is truly memorable, reflects your brand and helps you stand out from the crowd.

Once you have a strong visual identity, it should be applied to all of your brand communication media, online and offline, to ensure clarity and consistency. This chapter takes you through the steps of a BIO makeover, as it's transformed into a BRANDED BIO. To help you out, there are tips, tools and resources on layout, typography, fonts, colors and your headshot.

Why design is important for your BIO

A strong visual identity, applied consistently across all your online/offline media will help to establish you firmly in people's minds. This means using the same set of fonts, colors and imagery throughout your brand communications. Following the principles of good typography will give your BRANDED BIO a professional edge, and applying a distinctive design will stamp it with your unique visual brand to emphasize your differentiation.

FIVE Guidelines for a Distinctive BRANDED BIO

1. Typography
   • Be consistent. Use the Style palette to set up styles for Normal text, headings and other features and apply them consistently throughout your document.

- It's in the detail. Use "curly" quote marks rather than straight ones; increase line spacing to three points greater than the font size; reduce the depth of the blank line space between paragraphs to around 10 points; always use a bullet symbol or suitable "dingbat" (from a symbol font such as Zapf Dingbats, Wingdings or Webdings), rather than a hyphen in lists to help items stand out.

- Avoid underlining and overuse of caps. For emphasis, use bold or italics (judiciously), or select a different heading size to draw attention to a point.

- Avoid the common habit of two spaces after punctuation, especially if you choose to use justified text. It's a hangover from the days of typewriters and can create too many unsightly gaps in your text.

- Finally—and most importantly—proofread, proofread. Don't rely on your auto spell checker. Get somebody with writing skills to look at your BIO carefully. Nothing mars the overall effect more than poor spelling, punctuation and grammar. The person you most want to impress might be a real stickler for old-fashioned attention to detail!

2. **Design and layout**

- Allow *at least* three quarters of an inch (or 2 cms) side margins and half an inch (1.3 cms) top and bottom margins.

- Create two columns. The narrower one can be used for highlighting important information, your contact details and adding your company and association logos (obtain permission for their use).

- The placement of your headshot (if used) depends on which way your body is angled. Position it so that your head and/or body are angled into, rather than out of, the page.

- Don't be tempted to make the font size too small (10 or 11pt minimum, depending on the font used): it is preferable to reduce the word count, than make the copy difficult to read. If in doubt, ask someone you know who struggles with small print to give their opinion.

3. **Images**

- Ensure that logos, headshots and other graphics are high-resolution originals, not low resolution Web graphics copied from your website.

- Do not copy images or templates from the Internet unless it is clearly stated that their use is unrestricted. You can purchase images from stock libraries such as http://www.istockphoto.com that offer royalty-free photos and illustrations for a small fee.

- Avoid low-quality clip art, which can look amateurish.

4. **Fonts**

- Times New Roman is the default serif typeface in Microsoft Word, but has poor letter and word spacing. Adobe Garamond or Georgia are good alternatives.

- Helvetica, Verdana, and Arial are sans serif fonts used for headings, displays and for online purposes because they're more readable on screen. For narrow columns they're fine, but they're not really suitable for document-width text blocks.

- When choosing a font, stick to a clean classic that won't detract from your message. You can find a huge selection of fonts on http://www.myfonts.com. It has a feature to preview different fonts which can be sent as a collection to your designer to demonstrate your preferences.

- Converting your document to a PDF will ensure your fonts will display correctly, regardless of whether recipients have them on their computers or not. If your document is in Word, use standard fonts for compatibility.

5. Colors

In his recent article on color, William Arruda says: "Color is important for personal branding. Color can be used to express your personal brand attributes, evoke emotion, and build that all-important connection with people."

- For normal text, black is the best choice as it ensures a crisp, easy-to-read text. Very dark colors may also be used, providing there is sufficient contrast between text and background.

- Avoid colored boxes behind text, shadows and other font effects that can make your BIO look cluttered and messy.

- Print: saturated colors, especially in the blue spectrum, look fabulous on-screen, but do not always reproduce well in print. Print out your document to check how the colors look and make adjustments if necessary. Also try printing the document in grayscale and increase the contrast if the tones are too similar.

FIVE Guidelines for a Fabulous Headshot

When building a strong and compelling brand for yourself, quality professional photographs are essential and can make a big difference in how you are perceived. If you are communicating a message of quality, a professional portrait on your BIO will attract and reassure your readers and give you credibility.

It is well documented that people make up their minds about each other within the first few seconds of meeting. This first impression comprises a staggering 93% of the criteria they use when they form an opinion about others. The same applies to the initial impression of your BIO, including your photograph. Even the most beautifully crafted layout and copy can be let down by a poor headshot, yet many people use home snapshots which do them no justice at all.

Why do you need a headshot on your BRANDED BIO?

A good headshot is an opportunity for you to personalize your BIO. It helps build a picture of who you are and to establish a connection with your reader. If you want to make a terrific first impression, it pays to look your best.

NOTE: For a job application, it is wise to check whether you should include a headshot. Many recruiters, especially in North America, select interview applicants by their written credentials only.

---

1. **Find a good photographer**
   - Be prepared to invest in a professional photographer. This is not something to skimp on: the results will be worth the investment.

   - Research the photographer. Word of mouth is great as long as you can see examples of their work. Search the Internet and look at portfolios to get an idea of their style.

   - If using an amateur photographer, follow the tips below. Make sure you're in good natural light (flash can be very stark) and have plenty of shots taken so you can pick the best ones.

2. **Be well prepared**
   - Collect samples from magazines or websites to demonstrate the look you want.

   - Do a dress rehearsal at home in front of the mirror, practicing expressions and poses to find what suits you best.

   - Drink lots of water and get plenty of sleep beginning a few days prior to the photo shoot.

   - Avoid the temptation to try a new hairstyle or dress style. Your headshot should reflect the way you normally look at your best.

3. **Clothes, colors, and make-up tips:**

- Solid colors work best; avoid patterns and busy textures. Black is good, but it's best to avoid white unless it's underneath something. If you regularly receive compliments that you look good in a particular color, you can be sure it's one that flatters you.

- Dark clothes attract less attention—the focus should be on your face. Make sure your clothes are pressed and don't be tempted to overdress.

- Avoid jewelry that detracts from your face, and choose simple pieces that flatter you.

- If you already have a brand color palette, choose clothes and accessories that match or complement your branding. Take examples of your branding to help your photographer choose the right background colors.

- Make-up should be clean and natural—this isn't the time to try a new look.

- Ladies, wear a light foundation and emphasize eyes and lips.

- For both sexes, if you have a tendency to shine or an uneven complexion, translucent powder will help your face to appear flawless in photos. It will seem unnatural, but don't worry, the studio lighting will compensate. Professional studios may have make-up artists on hand to help you.

4. **What to take with you**

- A variety of tops and shirts, with a few accessories such as scarves or ties will give you and the photographer a chance to choose the best outfit. Have shots taken in different outfits to give you more choice when it comes to selecting a headshot for a particular purpose.

- Your previous headshots (gives the photographer something to improve on!)

5. **Design and placement considerations**

- Have shots taken with your body angled both left and right, with your face toward the camera. Don't look down your nose: it is more flattering to extend your chin slightly and look up at the camera.

- Having a choice of shots with your body angled either way allows you or your designer to select a headshot that will be orientated towards the centre of the page, rather than looking out of it.

- Ask the photographer to supply a choice of sizes. You need a high resolution (high definition) file to send to printers or magazine editors, and a selection of small sizes for use on the Internet. One or two cropped photos (where your head almost fills the frame) will be useful. See the Resources list for links to inspiring headshots.

Case Story of a BIO Make-over: Simone-Eva Redrupp

Simone-Eva Redrupp had a basic BIO that she used for networking, introductions and speaking engagements. Hastily put together, she had circulated her BIO sporadically. One recipient, a personal brand strategist who knew Simone-Eva well, commented that the content didn't adequately reflect her brand. It was missing contact information and her photo didn't do her justice. In general the recipient found the document "off-brand," especially for someone of Simone-Eva's high professional standing. Simone-Eva welcomed the feedback, agreed completely, and with her usual enthusiasm and energy decided to work with a personal brand strategist and designer to identify and clarify the written and visual communication of her personal brand.

The Before: Basic BIO with Headshot

Low resolution, poor contrast
headshot, taken from website

On wrong side
of page: the body
is angled outwards

Off-brand
"Comic Sans" font,
all capitals

SIMONE-EVA REDRUPP

Default
leading

Simone is a "third-culture person," educated in five countries on two continents, who has worked in 7 countries. She comes from the financial & hospitality services, and the consulting field, where she has held senior operational- key account management and marketing positions with multinationals (Aperian Global, Lufthansa German Airline, Club Med, Citibank, Disneyland Resort Paris in such countries as: France, Germany, USA, Mexico, Senegal, Austria, India, Belgium, etc.. .

An experienced Senior Facilitator, Trainer and Professor, she teaches, designs and facilitates international teambuilding and cross-cultural seminars for Fortune 500, CAC 40 multinational clients, as well as International Business Schools worldwide from Finland to Namibia, and from the USA to India. Coaching international managers to leverage cultural differences as an asset is her primary mission, in addition to helping multicultural teams improve their cross-border collaboration and overall team effectiveness in a global environment. Helping high potential future managers to lead, as well as become effective global members of international teams, is a key element of these workshops. She also continuously conducts and contributes to research on such topics as: global leadership, crosscultural effectiveness, diversity and inclusion, etc.

Simone-Eva holds a BA degree from *Rice University* (Houston, Texas), coursework from the *Albert Ludwigs Universität* in Germany, and an MBA/MIM (Master in International Management) from *The American Graduate School of International Management* (Thunderbird) in Phoenix, Arizona.

Tri-cultural, Simone-Eva resides in Paris, France from where she lectures, facilitates and researches worldwide in French, English and German.

Line space
between paragraphs

Double spaces
after punctuation

Wide text column,
sans serif font,
fully justified

Simone-Eva's basic BIO, with some of the mistakes highlighted:

- Poor headshot, badly positioned
- Unwise choice of fonts
- Full justification (text forced to fit paragraph width) which causes unattractive spaces between words on some lines
- Some double spacing after punctuation
- Wide column width is harder to read
- Spacing between lines and after paragraphs could be improved
- No contact details

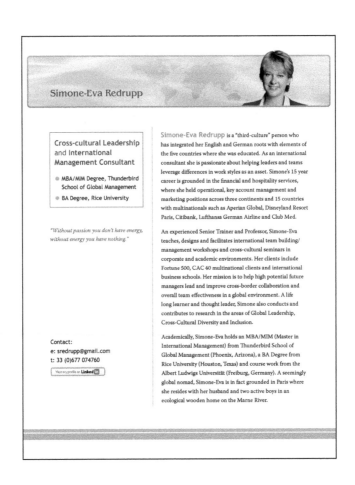

Simone-Eva Redrupp

Cross-cultural Leadership and International Management Consultant

- MBA/MIM Degree, Thunderbird School of Global Management
- BA Degree, Rice University

"Without passion you don't have energy, without energy you have nothing."

Contact:
e: sredrupp@gmail.com
t: 33 (0)677 074760

View my profile on Linked in

Simone-Eva Redrupp is a "third-culture" person who has integrated her English and German roots with elements of the five countries where she was educated. As an international consultant she is passionate about helping leaders and teams leverage differences in work styles as an asset. Simone's 15 year career is grounded in the financial and hospitality services, where she held operational, key account management and marketing positions across three continents and 15 countries with multinationals such as Aperian Global, Disneyland Resort Paris, Citibank, Lufthansa German Airline and Club Med.

An experienced Senior Trainer and Professor, Simone-Eva teaches, designs and facilitates international team building/ management workshops and cross-cultural seminars in corporate and academic environments. Her clients include Fortune 500, CAC 40 multinational clients and international business schools. Her mission is to help high potential future managers lead and improve cross-border collaboration and overall team effectiveness in a global environment. A life long learner and thought leader, Simone also conducts and contributes to research in the areas of Global Leadership, Cross-Cultural Diversity and Inclusion.

Academically, Simone-Eva holds an MBA/MIM (Master in International Management) from Thunderbird School of Global Management (Phoenix, Arizona), a BA Degree from Rice University (Houston, Texas) and course work from the Albert Ludwigs Universität (Freiburg, Germany). A seemingly global nomad, Simone-Eva is in fact grounded in Paris where she resides with her husband and two active boys in an ecological wooden home on the Marne River.

After committing to the personal branding process, Simone-Eva now has the above BRANDED BIO with an impactful visual identity that can be applied consistently to all her brand communications: business card, PowerPoint template, letterhead, professional site, Twitter background, white paper, video BIO, resume, and more.

This BRANDED BIO makeover shows how visual branding and a few key changes to the layout make the entire document more inviting. The banner image is not too overpowering, and gives a quick visual reference to one of Simone-Eva's key attributes—her global brand. The text is presented in two columns, the left column can be used for alumni, association or company logos, LinkedIn, FaceBook, Twitter link, quotes, testimonials or other visuals. Simone-Eva chose to add her LinkedIn link button (which is clickable in the PDF) and a quote.

Here are some examples of how Simone-Eva's branding can be applied on a PowerPoint template, business card, and website:

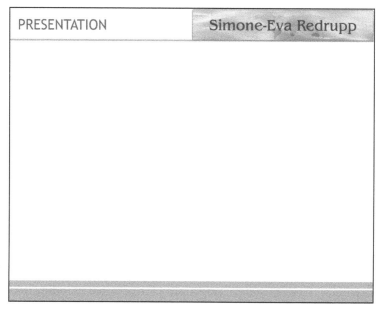

Simone-Eva Redrupp

HOME   BIOGRAPHY   CONTACT

Cross-cultural Leadership and International Management Consultant

- MBA/MIM Degree, Thunderbird School of Global Management

- BA Degree, Rice University

View my profile on Linked in

"Without passion you don't have energy, without energy you have nothing."

Simone-Eva Redrupp is a "third-culture" person who has integrated her English and German roots with elements of the five countries where she was educated. As an international consultant she is passionate about helping leaders and teams leverage differences in work styles as an asset. Simone's 15 year career is grounded in the financial and hospitality services, where she held operational, key account management and marketing positions across three continents and 15 countries with multinationals such as Aperian Global, Disneyland Resort Paris, Citibank, Lufthansa German Airline and Club Med.

An experienced Senior Trainer and Professor, Simone-Eva teaches, designs and facilitates international team building/management workshops and cross-cultural seminars in corporate and academic environments. Her clients include Fortune 500, CAC 40 multinational clients and international business schools. Her mission is to help high potential future managers lead and improve cross-border collaboration and overall team effectiveness in a global environment. A life long learner and thought leader, Simone also conducts and contributes to research in the areas of Global Leadership, Cross-Cultural Diversity and Inclusion.

Academically, Simone-Eva holds an MBA/MIM (Master in International Management) from Thunderbird School of Global Management (Phoenix, Arizona), a BA Degree from Rice University (Houston, Texas) and course work from the Albert Ludwigs Universität (Freiburg, Germany). A seemingly global nomad, Simone-Eva is in fact grounded in Paris where she resides with her husband and two active boys in an ecological wooden home on the Marne River.

BIO

Sue Brettell is the go-to creative passionista for personal branding design and copy. A Preferred Personal Branding Strategist with Reach, she focuses on branded new media and Wordpress Web design for dynamic professionals and executives driven to make a positive impact in the world. Sue is creatively versatile, tech-savvy, innovative and intuitive, with exquisite attention to detail. She combines years of training and experience in multidisciplinary design, publishing and personal development to provide well-crafted visual identities and copy that effectively leverage her clients' unique value propositions. A visionary entrepreneur, Sue lives in Suffolk, UK and works with clients around the globe.

Sue Brettell http://www.suebrettell.com
Personal Branding Designer and Copywriter

Links and Resources

Typography
http://www.desktoppub.about.com/od/typography—a very comprehensive resource if you want to dig deeper.

Headshot examples
http://www.helenbartlett.co.uk/headshots—this is a lovely portfolio of natural headshots to give you some ideas.

http://studiomark.com/corporate-headshots.html—scroll down the page to see a good selection of headshots. Note that they differ in style to suit the sitters' professions.

http://www.deborahmeaden.com—Ms. Meaden is a highly successful entrepreneur and her headshots reflect her laser-sharp, no-nonsense style. Note that they are well placed on the page.

http://www.trumpuniversity.com/blog—as you would expect, Donald Trump demonstrates excellent use of headshots on his beautifully designed blog.

Designers (these sites are good sources for locating freelance designers)
http://www.Elance.com
http://www.GetAFreelancer.com
http://www.Guru.com

Fonts
http://www.MyFonts.com
http://www.UrbanFonts.com

Color
http://www.Visibone.com/colorlab—very easy to pick colors and get their references.
http://www.Websitetips.com/colorcharts/visibone/hex
http://www.Degraeve.com/color-palette—generate a color palette from a photo.

Disclaimer: the links, and references made, are correct at time of print. Due to the changeable nature of the Internet, no responsibility is taken for changes to URLs or content, especially regarding placement of headshots. A Web search will provide plenty of links to sites offering fonts and image galleries.

BIO GEMS

GEMS consist of content that is woven into your story and that elicits and messages a warm, humorous, memorable or captivating "touch point." This can be by referencing one's childhood, a hero, mentor, influencer or through the use of quotes. Examples are given in the form of excerpts from BIOS of consultants, professionals, entrepreneurs, artists, designers and coaches as found on their LinkedIn profile, company or personal site. In most cases a link is provided to read, as Paul Harvey would say, the "rest of the story" i.e., in its full context. Think of the GEMS to craft about your story that will make you memorable and stand out.

Mentor, Influencer, or Hero Reference:

Kristen Jacoway—Founder of Career Design Coach, LLC

(excerpt) Combine career-counseling expertise, an empathetic nature, and a lifelong interest in technology, and what do you get? Meet Kristen Jacoway, Career Design Coach. The seeds of Kristen's calling were planted in her youth, beginning with the strong work ethic instilled in her by her parents. When she was in middle school, her father, now retired Charter NASA rocket scientist Gene Austin, brought home a Macintosh computer, and Kristen embarked on a journey of discovery. Kristen's dad continually upgraded to stay abreast of cutting-edge technology over the years, and each wave of innovation provided a fresh opportunity for Kristen to develop a level of knowledge and skill uncommon among her contemporaries.

Read the rest of Kristen's Story here http://www.kristenjacoway.com.

Dzintra Dzenis—Executive Chef and Owner at Plate by Dzintra

I was influenced, first and foremost by my Mom, second by Julia Child (a fellow alumnus), and third by my 20 years of life in France. There, I had the opportunity to feast from the most amazing farmers markets and some of the most brilliant culinary tables of the world, which by the way, I often found at the unsuspected neighborhood bistro.

Today, I am a classically trained Chef in French Cuisine and Pastry from the Cordon Bleu in Paris. Although French culinary techniques form the basis of my culinary point of view, my strength lies in French Fusion cuisine. Using only the freshest, preferably local, and predominantly seasonal ingredients, I borrow from flavors and other culinary techniques from around the world, to introduce anyone with a sense of adventure to a lighter and more diversified style of cooking with plenty of sensuality and boldness. My food will never neglect a single part of your palette.

Read the rest of Dzintra's story here http://www.platebydzintra.com.

Samuel Kone—Marketing Consultant

(excerpt) Inspired by the examples of his grandfather, of his own father's social and political activism, of Berry Gordy, founder of Motown records and of Mohammad Yunus, Samuel has the hope of becoming, like his heroes, a bridge contributing his own unifying vision and unique perspective to the North-South economic, racial, and social divide.

Quote Reference:

Weaving quotes into your storytelling is an excellent way to illuminate your narratives. The source can be you...what you often say, your mantra, a favorite quote (anonymous or not), or what others say about you (reference letters, 360°, testimonials or evaluations). Looking for inspirational quotes that resonate with your brand? On Google, type in QUOTES, and a host of sites will surface.

(excerpt) Pamela's favorite quote by Albert Einstein is "Try not to become a man of success but rather to become a man of value." In her own words this means that individual notoriety or fame is secondary. It is rather bringing added value to the organization, employing full commitment to the project at hand, and ultimately leading to the successful completion of objectives.

(excerpt) Tom's commitment to add value to the organization was recognized by his manager who described him as "a deeply involved, reliable, accurate and tenacious professional. He demonstrates leadership thanks to a strong competency and perfect knowledge of his projects."

(excerpt) Recognized formally as a leader adept at empowering and influencing others, what is more revealing are words from colleagues and team members describing David as "focused with a strong ability to convince people and instill confidence. He communicates clearly, setting distinct goals and exudes enthusiasm and confidence."

Weave in Passions, Personal Social Responsibility (PSR), Volunteer Activities, Values, Interests, and Childhood Memories

Scott Hoyle—Artist

(excerpt) Scott Hoyle sees the world through a colored lens, and exudes his creativity through everything he does—painting, photography, illustration and graphic design. Many young boys, when asked what they want to be when they grow up, answer "fireman" or "policeman." But Scott was known to see and think differently, and with his head held high he always proudly answered, "I'm going to be an artist." Although the typical response was, "No, what are you going to do for a REAL job?," Scott never wavered from his passionate commitment. Rather than frogs and slingshots in his pockets, you would be more apt to find a doodling tool of any type. Filled with curiosity and wonder, Scott spent every spare minute drawing, and by the third grade he could already draw over 25 unique cartoon characters!

Read the rest of Scott's story here http://www.scotthoyle.com.

Maren Finzer—Personal Brand Strategist

(excerpt) Maren's creativity, pursuit of excellence, and enthusiastic entrepreneurial spirit began as a young girl, being born to, and strongly influenced by, two passionate business-minded parents. Maren's father taught her, at a young age, the importance of integrating work and personal life. He was an early pioneer of international banking. Traveling the world for US Bank, he managed the financing of all the imports and exports for businesses based in Oregon. It was the norm for him to bring his international clients home for an all-American dinner when they were in town. While Maren's friends were off together watching Brady Bunch, she was at home immersed in learning how to relate and connect to build diverse business relationships. She vividly remembers entertaining and engaging international guests in dinner conversation the best she could, despite the language barriers.

Read the rest of Maren's story here http://www.marenfinzer.com.

Karyn Craven—Designer and Founder of Burning Torch

Designer Karyn Craven was born and raised in Los Angeles, the second of six children. Encouraged by entrepreneurial parents, her creative skills were developed in childhood and nurtured through alternative education at small private schools. Craven had dreams of being an artist for as long as she can remember; dreams influenced by a love of nature, a respect for world cultures and history. In some ways, Craven's creation of Burning Torch as a "melting pot" of energies reflects her own hybrid nature formed through her large family and a heritage that combines Maltese, Scottish, English, Dutch and French cultures.

Read the rest of Karyn's story here http://www.burningtorchinc.com.

Weaving in Metaphors and Analogies

Randi Bussin, Founder and President, Aspire!

(Excerpt) Working with individuals in career renewal and reinvention is similar to the art and culture of growing bonsai, a hobby Randi has pursued for more than 20 years. Whether working with these inspirational trees or her clients, Randi's technique includes a unique combination of common sense and practicality, a touch of artistic expression, creative visioning, and artful experimentation for growth and renewal.

Read the rest of Randi's story here http://www.aspireforsuccess.com.

Humor

Erin Yoshimura, Founder—Empowerful Changes

(excerpt) Erin Yoshimura is all about empowerment and challenges her clients with wasabi wit and cultural compassion to find their voice and stand with vigor through emotional intelligence training, personal branding and career coaching.

Read the rest of Erin's story here http://www.empowerfulchanges.com.

The BIO Depot

The BIO DEPOT or BIO DUMP is the ultimate "catch all," a comprehensive holding tank to amass all of the information from this book. The purpose is to keep all the elements of your storytelling in one place. In keeping a dumping ground you are ready to cut, paste and tweak as needed and voila...a new version emerges. The BIO is a living, evolving document. You will be surprised at how fast multiple versions of your BIO start to surface as you will tailor based on usage, placement and target, and as new information accumulates.

The messaging and content you create about the "Brand Called You" will be used not only in various versions but will naturally flow into interview situations, your elevator pitch and a multitude of opportunities where you are "telling your story." This is not a static document but will evolve and grow over time as you add more components and integrate the "mini-stories," quotes, references, and testimonials. Each time you start to put together a version...FIRST consider the TARGET and pick and choose elements and a structure and flow that is appropriate...ALWAYS use a fresh approach. Think of ways to make it more appealing with more impact and resonance. Using this BIO DEPOT tool, it is important to insert every new version and document the date, placement and usage. This will avoid "re-creating the wheel"...all you do is "change the spokes." Happy Storytelling!

BIO Log: (add more rows as you add more versions)

Date	Word Count	Placement/Usage	BIO content

Summary/Profile Statement on Your Resume	
Assessments	Indicate key findings, outcomes, results, indicators
Quotes	These can be your favorites, from recognized sources or anonymous, or your own
Visibility Branding Storytelling	Add your well structured accomplishment stories here
References	Add any testimonials, evaluations, endorsements, quotes and LinkedIn recommendations
Personal Social Responsibility (PSR)	List volunteer activities, social projects, donations, philanthropic initiatives, other...

Action Verbs

Achieved	Contributed	Expedited	Mobilized	Repaired
Acquired	Controlled	Formulated	Moderated	Researched
Acted	Coordinated	Fostered	Modernized	Reshaped
Adjusted	Corrected	Generated	Monitored	Restructured
Administered	Counseled	Grouped	Motivated	Reversed
Advised	Created	Guided	Negotiated	Reviewed
Analyzed	Customized	Headed	Obtained	Revised
Applied	Decentralized	Helped	Opened	Saved
Approved	Decided	Hired	Operated	Scheduled
Arranged	Decreased	Identified	Organized	Selected
Assembled	Defined	Implemented	Participated	Serviced
Assigned	Delegated	Improved	Performed	Simplified
Assisted	Delivered	Increased	Persuaded	Sold
Attained	Demonstrated	Indexed	Planned	Solved
Budgeted	Designed	Influenced	Prepared	Spearheaded
Built	Developed	Initiated	Presented	Specified
Calculated	Diagnosed	Inspected	Presided	Standardized
Catalogued	Directed	Installed	Produced	Started up
Centralized	Distributed	Instituted	Programmed	Stimulated
Chaired	Doubled	Instructed	Projected	Strengthened

Classified	Downsized	Integrated	Promoted	Structured
Coached	Drafted	Intensified	Proposed	Summarized
Communicated	Edited	Interpreted	Provided	Supervised
Compiled	Encouraged	Introduced	Purchased	Systematized
Completed	Enhanced	Invented	Recommended	Trained
Composed	Enlarged	Investigated	Reconciled	Transferred
Computed	Ensured	Launched	Recruited	Transformed
Conceived	Established	Led	Rectified	Translated
Conducted	Estimated	Maintained	Reduced	Turned
Consolidated	Evaluated	Managed	Refocused	Turned around
Constructed	Examined	Marketed	Renegotiated	Upgraded
Consulted	Exceeded	Mediated	Renovated	Verified
Contracted	Expanded	Merged	Reorganized	Wrote

Conclusion

his book has taken you on a voyage to strengthen your brand in this constantly evolving world. I hope it has given you a fresh perspective on how to trigger the stories and create GEMS that will delight your target. In making you aware of new areas to explore, your stories will resonate with more people, in more places. Never underestimate the power of a good story and now having come to the end of the book, you are better equipped to answer the question...

So, what's your Story????

Visibility Branding offers sessions and workshops on Personal Branding, Online Identity, Storytelling and BIO Development to individuals and groups in virtual and on-site environments. Founder, Bernadette Martin is also available for speaking engagements and keynote presentations.
Contact: bmartin@visibilitybranding.com
Site: http://www.visibilitybranding.com

Afterword by Jason Alba

By the time I got to this point in the book my head was spinning. I've watched Bernadette go through various renditions of this book and I've seen it mature into what it is today, which is an exceptional resource and guide to help you come up with your story.

Here's what I'd suggest: Get out a sheet of paper and list the D-words down the side. Then, make notes and action items on each one so you can start the process. Do it step-by-step so you aren't overwhelmed. I think you'll get two things from going through this exercise:

First, you'll have your story, and versions of your story (including mini-bios) ready for many different situations. This will pay off for years to come. Opportunities will arise that you don't know about yet, but when they ask "can you send us some information about yourself," you can confidently send them your well-crafted, strategic, on-brand and compelling story.

Second, going through this process will help you understand yourself, your passions, your strengths, and your direction better. You may find there are things you didn't realize you did so well, or patterns and trends you didn't realize you gravitate towards, that might change the trajectory of your career. It sounds a little absurd to think that you don't know yourself well right now, but going through this process might uncover, or validate, things that you haven't critically thought about.

Get to work and you'll benefit many times over as you use your story online and offline.

Jason Alba
Author of *I'm on LinkedIn—Now What???*
CEO and creator of JibberJobber.com

Contributors

A huge MERCI (*mille fois*) to the contributors who added their insights, knowledge, expertise, and perspectives to this book. Following is the list in alphabetical order, of this valued and prestigious group. BIOS and photos can be viewed at http://www.visibilitybranding.com (speaking of photos, special thanks to Rob Sitbon for my headshots).

Jason Alba, Founder
JibberJobber
http://www.JibberJobber.com

William Arruda, Founder
Reach Communications
http://www.reachcc.com

Pierre Blanc, Micro Finance Advocate
http://www.pierreblanc.org

Lou Bortone, Founder
Online Video Branding, LLC
http://www.OnlineVideoBranding.com

Sue Brettell
Personal Branding Designer & Copywriter
http://www.suebrettell.com

Angel Cabrera, President
Thunderbird School of Global Management
http://www.thunderbird.edu

Rebecca Castleton, Founder
Castleton and Associates
http://www.castletonassociates.com

Paul Copcutt, Founder
Square Peg Solution
http://www.squarepegsolution.com

Karyn Craven, Founder
Burning Torch
http://www.burningtorchinc.com

Dzintra Dzenis, Chef
Plate by Dzintra
http://www.platebydzintra.com

Fabio Ferrari, Executive
http://www.fabioferrari.eu

Megan Fitzgerald, Founder
Career by Choice
http://www.careerbychoice.com

Amy Grossman, Founder
Broader Vision
http://www.broadervision.com

Susan Guarneri, Assessment Goddess
http://www.AssessmentGoddess.com

Cecile Hasroyan, Image Consultant
http://www.cecileh.com

Diana Jennings, Founder
Brand You Image
http://www.brandyouimage.com

Sandrine Joseph, Talent Management Director
http://fr.linkedin.com/in/sandrinejoseph

Alexander Kumming, Founder
Strong Education and MBACube
http://www.mbacube.com

Mitchell Levy, Founder
Happy About
http://www.happyabout.info

Cathy Altman Nocquet, Book Editor
http://fr.linkedin.com/in/cathyaltmannocquet

Simone-Eva Redrupp, Consultant
http://fr.linkedin.com/pub/simone-eva-redrupp-durand/3/142/b20

Annalisa Riches, Senior European HR Business Partner
http://fr.linkedin.com/pub/annalisa-riches/1/399/855

Barbara Safani, Owner
Career Solvers
http://www.careersolvers.com

Rob Sitbon, Video Photographer
http://www.robsitbon.com

Serge Soudoplatoff, Founder
HYPERDOXE
http://www.hyperdoxe.net

Lynda Sydney, Copywriter
http://www.lyndasydney.com

Julie Vetter, Technology Director
Branding Salon
http://www.julievetter.com

Susan Weinschenk, PhD Psychology
http://www.whatmakesthemclick.net

Erin Yoshimura, Founder
Empowerful Changes
http://www.empowerfulchanges.com

Meet the Author

Bernadette Martin, Founder of Visibility Branding, LLC is a certified Personal Brand Strategist, Author, Speaker, and Entrepreneur. Intrigued by the art of storytelling and by nature a good listener, intuitive and curious about people, Bernadette loves to help individuals develop their personal brand and message it in a compelling way, both online and offline. After a 15-year international corporate career working with many Fortune 500 brands, she transitioned in 2003 to working with personal brands where she offers career development services for individuals, corporations and organizations in virtual and on-site environments. Corporate, academic and individual clients are connected to leading brands such as Cisco, Chanel, Goldman Sachs, Orange, Cordon Bleu, Mercedes, IBM, INSEAD, IMD and HEC. In addition to speaking engagements, she hosts and produces the Visibility Branding Webinar Series where she gives online training and also interviews guest speakers—authors and experts—to discuss topics related to career development. Participants join her from around the world.

Bernadette is multi-lingual with an MBA from Thunderbird, School of Global Management and certification as a Reach Personal Brand Strategist, Online Identity Expert and 360°Reach Assessment Analyst. Fully aware of the value of giving to her networks, Bernadette is a Board Member of her Alumni Association and President of the French chapter, recent Vice President of the American University Clubs of France, and an active member of the European Professional Women's Network.

Originally from Los Angeles, Bernadette is of Irish, German, and French descent. She considers herself to be truly "Euro-American" with an early interest in cross-cultural experiences and foreign languages. A runner who has completed several marathons, she has a preference for mountain running with favorite trails in the Canadian Rockies, the French Alps, Taipei and the Grand Canyon. Her favorite quote is a Tibetan proverb, "Happiness is not at the end of the road, it's the road that brings happiness." In her own words she would say it is not the "fait accompli" that matters but the excitement, fun and challenges the road (even if it's uphill) presents in getting there.

More Praise for
Storytelling about Your Brand Online & Offline

"'In her book, Bernadette advocates using LinkedIn and alumni association sites. I agree with her that posting an engaging profile is key to connecting. The Thunderbird alumni association is a strong and globally active community. The connections made through our site, My T-Bird, remain pure to Thunderbird. Posting a BIO allows alumni to tell the Thunderbird community the story of their journey to where they are today and is a valuable tool for them to introduce or re-introduce themselves to prospective business partners, employers and friends."
Aleksandra Lubavs, President of the Thunderbird Alumni Network Board

"In her timely book, Bernadette, recent Vice President of Communication of the American University Clubs of France (AUC), shows the usefulness of writing an effective BIO or story for networking and profile placement purposes. I share her excellent advice with the members of the more than 25 alumni associations."
Aurelien Cottet, President of the American University Clubs of France

"As a jazz and gospel singer, composer, lyricist, and author, I am often called upon to tailor performances and conferences with complimentary bios for special occasions. One standard BIO does not suit every situation. For this reason Martin's suggestion of a BIO Depot or "BIO Dump" strikes me as especially relevant for artists and musicians who do not rely on traditional bios to sell their brand. BIO bits saved in our personal depot from here and there provide a wealth of thoughts at our proverbial fingertips when needed. Kudos for Martin's clear and incisive look at the why, the how, and wherefore of Branding."

Manda Djinn, Jazz and Gospel Singer, Composer, Lyricist and Author
http://mandadjinn.free.fr, http://www.myspace.com/mandadjinn

"This book is a definite "must read" for those of us who are willing to take a long look at themselves and to then make the required changes in order to develop and refine their own brands. You will get all the help you need to work through the steps to making sure that what you project to the world is indeed what you "want" to project. Bernadette Martin writes well and uses simple, very descriptive examples which give clarity to the process of developing and changing. I especially like the section on Storytelling, which incidentally, commercial brands have been using successfully for years and which in Ms. Martin's language become personal and very powerful tools for creating "my/your/our" brands. But more than anything else I think that the encouragement to "self awareness" makes this book one of the most valuable and very useful and re-readable books on my bookshelf!"

Donya Ekstrand - Marketing & Communications Manager, Ericsson AB, Stockholm, Sweden

"We know that generational success for the family business is enhanced by inspirational storytelling about our founder (my grandfather), his principles and values. This helps forge human connections and instill loyalty from both inside and outside our company enabling the Tauck World Discovery brand to flourish for three generations. With insights that ring true, page after page, Ms. Martin strategizes and contemporizes the storytelling tradition, which is so highly relevant within our globalized online economy today."

Robin Tauck, Owner and past CEO - Tauck World Discovery
Board Member: World Travel & Tourism Council; United States Travel Association

"We waited far too long for this book. Now it's here—a book that contains breathtaking insights and thoroughly explains the forces of personal branding. With a systematic and stringent logic in her approach, with simplicity and clarity in her writing, the author leads us right to the essence of the issues. "Storytelling about Your Brand" offers an innovative perspective and practical guidance on one of the most important topics in brand stewardship and personal development. In all the previous research for my publications like "Strategy for personal development", "le CV international" or "Talent Management" I would have loved a source like this book. I'm thankful to Bernadette that she now shares her expertise and experience with us. Read it. You will be fascinated and stimulated to create, nurture and grow your individual personal brand."

Edgar C. Britschgi, M.A./MBA, President - British Swiss Chamber of Commerce Zurich/London
Managing Partner, Combo Management AG, Zug, New York, Shanghai, Taipei and Tel Aviv

"I have been a Human Resources manager for more than a decade. I have interviewed literally hundreds of candidates, in nine countries, for positions ranging from Chauffeur to Public Diplomacy Specialist, from Scientist to Financial Management clerk. And those who were the most compelling were the ones who, rather than approach the interview in the traditional manner of giving a laundry list of accomplishments, had real stories to tell. The stellar candidates, the gold that shone through the dross, were those who dressed up their experiences, and their lessons learned, in captivating stories that demonstrated for me their true self, the key aspects of their personality that would make them an excellent employee. The true beauty of Bernadette's book is that it drives this message home with clarity and dexterity, showing the reader how to prepare for an interview in a way that gives them a real advantage in the job interview process. Having this knowledge could very well be the difference between finding yourself courted by Human Resource managers and never getting that call back."

Bill Michael, Director of Human Resources - US Missions to France

"Have you have ever yearned for clear, foolproof instructions on how to build that famous "elevator pitch" you know you're supposed to have? Or have you thought you should be asking your contacts for recommendations on LinkedIn but didn't quite know how? Or have you ever silently agreed that yes, OK, you need to market "the Brand Called You" but just didn't know how to begin? Bernadette guides the reader through the process, exploring the connections and distinctions that exist between the plethora of online and offline tools and providing clear guidelines on how to get started. This valuable book shows the links between Web-based applications and the more traditional "offline" ways candidates use to communicate with employers (and vice versa) such as face-to-face interviewing and in-person networking. Guess what–it all starts with good old storytelling techniques that are easy to learn! The days when only CEOs and top management required a branded BIO and an Internet presence are gone–everyone needs to understand and use these powerful tools."
Danielle Savage, Career Counselor - American University of Paris

"Toastmasters has nearly 250,000 members in 106 countries seeking to develop and perfect their communication and leadership skills. Storytelling is part of the Toastmasters curriculum, and for storytelling, Bernadette Martin is a pro. Her book presents the reader with excellent techniques and tools. I've seen Bernadette captivate an audience with her charisma and her unique concept of professional and personal branding. With this book I have realized that storytelling, which is a skill that I apply often with my children, also applies to adult development and the business environment."
Nicolas Stricher, President 2009–2010, Toastmasters Busy Professionals, France

The Kiva Story

Making the world a better place: Bernadette Martin's Kiva story

Kiva is a non-profit organization with the mission of connecting people to alleviate poverty through lending. By combining micro finance with the internet, Kiva has created a caring, financial community of tens of thousands, facilitating over $100 million in loans to entrepreneurs around the world.

Kiva was the designated organization for fundraising at the 2007 Brand You World Telesummit. There, Bernadette Martin interviewed Kiva's Director of Public Relations. Inspired by how many beliefs and values she shared with the organization, Bernadette became a Kiva lender and Brand Ambassador.

To further her effort, the author will make a Kiva loan possible for every 50 copies of her book that are sold. Over time, as these loans are repaid, more entrepreneurs will be financed. The photos and BIOs or stories of each entrepreneur helped will appear on her site:
http://www.visibilitybranding.com

Kiva values and beliefs:

- People are by nature generous, and will help others if given the opportunity to do so in a transparent, accountable way.

- The poor are highly motivated and can be very successful when given an opportunity.

- By connecting people we can create relationships beyond financial transactions, and build a global community expressing support and encouragement of one another.

Kiva has the support of Oprah Winfrey, Maria Shriver and Bill Clinton. Go to http://www.kiva.org to see the photos and read the stories of some of the entrepreneurs in need. You can then respond to those that most resonate with you.

loans that change lives

Other Happy About® Books

Purchase these books at Happy About http://happyabout.info or at other online and physical bookstores.

JASON ALBA
FOREWORD BY BOB BURG

I'm on LinkedIn—Now What???

This book is designed to help you get the most out this popular business networking site.

Paperback $19.95
eBook $14.95

I'M IN A JOB SEARCH
Now What???

KRISTEN JACOWAY
FOREWORD BY JASON ALBA

I'm in a Job Search—Now What???

The book provides 100+ resources and tips to guide you through the job searching process to help you stand apart from your competition.

Paperback $19.95
eBook $14.95